ENGLISH DRAMATISTS

Series Editor:
Bruce King

ENGLISH DRAMATISTS
Series Editor: Bruce King

Published titles

Richard Cave, *Ben Jonson*
Christine Richardson and Jackie Johnston, *Medieval Drama*
Roger Sales, *Christopher Marlowe*
Katharine Worth, *Sheridan and Goldsmith*

Forthcoming titles

Susan Bassnett, *Shakespeare: Elizabethan Plays*
Laura Bromley, *Webster and Ford*
John Bull, *Vanbrugh and Farquhar*
Philip McGuire, *Shakespeare: Jacobean Plays*
Kate McLuskie, *Dekker and Heywood*
Max Novak, *Fielding and Gay*
David Thomas, *William Congreve*
Cheryl Turner, *Early Women Dramatists*
Albert Wertheim, *Etherege and Wycherley*
Martin White, *Middleton and Tourneur*

ENGLISH DRAMATISTS

SHERIDAN
and
GOLDSMITH

Katharine Worth
Emeritus Professor of Drama and
Theatre Studies in the
University of London

First published 1992 by
THE MACMILLAN PRESS LTD
Houndmills, Basingstoke, Hampshire RG21 2XS
and London
Companies and representatives
throughout the world

ISBN 0–333–44610–0 hardcover
ISBN 0–333–44611–9 paperback

A catalogue record for this book is available
from the British Library.

Printed and bound by Antony Rowe Ltd, Eastbourne

For Christopher, Elizabeth
and Charles, and Caroline, who typed it

Note on Quotations

Quotations from *She Stoops to Conquer*, *The Rivals*, *The Critic* and *The School for Scandal* are from the New Mermaids editions of these plays; *The Good Natur'd Man* from *Oliver Goldsmith: Two Plays*, the remaining Sheridan plays from *Sheridan's Plays*, ed. Cecil Price (which retains eighteenth-century spelling and punctuation).

Contents

Acknowledgements

Like all writers on Sheridan and Goldsmith, I owe a debt of gratitude to Cecil Price and Arthur Friedman for their definitive editions of the plays, and the wealth of information they have provided about them. I should like to thank the editors in the New Mermaids series and elsewhere for the excellently presented texts of individual plays used for quotation in this study. Thanks also to the actors and directors who have brought the texts to vivid life in productions such as those of Peter Wood at the National Theatre, London. These demonstrations of the plays in performance have been indispensable to my reading of the two playwrights.

Editor's Preface

Each generation needs to be introduced to the culture and great works of the past and to reinterpret them in its own ways. This series re-examines the important English dramatists of earlier centuries in the light of new information, new interests and new attitudes. The books are written for students, theatre-goers and general readers who want an up-to-date view of the plays and dramatists, with emphasis on drama as theatre and on stage, social and political history. Attention is given to what is known about performance, acting styles, changing interpretations, the stages and theatres of the time and theatre economics. The books will be relevant to those interested in or studying literature, theatre and cultural history.

BRUCE KING

Engraving of the scream scene from *The School for Scandal*

1
Sheridan and Goldsmith: Heavenly Twins

Sheridan and Goldsmith – it sounds a duo, almost a pairing of interchangeables like Tom Stoppard's Ros and Guil in *Rosencrantz and Guildenstern are Dead*. It is not really so, needless to say. Sheridan and Goldsmith are utterly distinct and distinctive as playwrights, let alone as men. Yet they do have a great deal in common, more than enough to justify their being discussed at least partly in tandem. Both were Irishmen, born in Ireland of Irish parents, yet making their careers and fame in England. Sheridan was brought to England by his family as a child of eight (and given an English upbringing, including schooling at Harrow). Goldsmith came to London on his own initiative, settling there as a young man in his twenties, after studying at Trinity College, Dublin (and Edinburgh), and spending some colourful 'wander' years in various parts of Europe.

Although there were twenty years between them, in terms of their theatre careers they were quite close contemporaries, who had many interests and attitudes in common. They hit their high point in the English theatre within a year or two of each other. Goldsmith's masterpiece, *She Stoops to Conquer*, had its first production at Covent Garden on 15 March 1773. It was followed at the same theatre, on 17 January 1775, by *The Rivals*. One brilliant Irishman succeeded another as though taking over the torch from

1

the compatriot who was obliged to leave the scene (Goldsmith died in the year of Sheridan's debut). Sheridan kept close to his predecessor in various ways, as will be seen.

In character the differences between the two are obvious, not least in the contrast of their conversational powers. Sheridan was as renowned for the irresistible charm and vivacity of his talk as Goldsmith for his clumsiness in conversation. Yet despite differences, they had something in common in personality as well as circumstance. Both had a blithe, feckless strain and were careless though generous with money. Goldsmith was an inveterate, unlucky gambler; Sheridan spent money like water and was erratic about paying bills, even – or perhaps especially – when managing Drury Lane. For years, only his privileged position as an MP protected him from arrest for debt (which caught up with him in the end). Goldsmith was equally well acquainted with the menace of bailiffs which he put to good comic use in his first play. Both could write at great speed, a gift they needed, being also great procrastinators. Stories abound of their troubles with deadlines. A taste for drink was a particular plague for Sheridan, getting out of control in his later years.

They also shared an unusual plenitude of talents, perhaps one reason for their easy attitude to responsibilities. They seemed able to triumph in any artistic occupation they took up and engaged successfully to a major extent in professional activities other than the theatre. While such mobility might not be unusual among minor playwrights, needing to turn their hand to anything for a living, it may strike us as odd that the theatre occupied so small a part in the *oeuvre* and lives of two such masters of comedy.

This was especially true of Goldsmith, who gained his immortality in the theatre on the strength of one play, after having written only one other. Most of his imaginative energy went into other forms of writing. He became the master of any genre with remarkable speed and ease, acquiring fame in his lifetime as poet, novelist and essayist as well as playwright. In fact it was as poet and novelist that he was best known for a time, a situation reflected in the critical commentaries on his life and work brought together in 1974 by G. S. Rousseau (*Critical Heritage* series): the reception of the plays occupies small space in this collection. Goldsmith could turn without apparent effort from the work required of a jobbing journalist and scholar, which was how he started literary life in

London, to the writing of a long poem (*The Traveller*) which Dr Johnson thought the best thing of the kind since Pope. He then won a whole new reputation with an immensely popular novel, *The Vicar of Wakefield*, and another long poem, *The Deserted Village*. Writing for the theatre involved a bigger jump, but even there, one apprentice work, *The Good Natur'd Man*, was all the preparation he needed before producing a comic masterpiece in *She Stoops to Conquer*.

Goldsmith died early, in his forties, so we cannot draw too many conclusions from the pattern of his *oeuvre* as we have it. Who knows but that he would have gone on to write more frequently for the theatre. From this same point of view, Sheridan's is a stranger case. His imaginative talent was entirely for drama; he was professionally committed to the theatre as a manager; he understood and loved the art of the actors. He might have been expected, despite his procrastination, to be a more prolific playwright.

Yet his theatrical career was curiously brief. Its great achievement was concentrated into a golden period of no more than four years, from 1775 to 1779 (modern taste would almost certainly exclude the declamatory *Pizarro* of 1799 which eighteenth-century audiences ranked as another triumph). When in 1775, at Covent Garden, the phenomenally successful *The Duenna* closed a year that had started with *The Rivals*, it was not surprising that the great Garrick, then on the point of retiring, should offer to the young playwright a major share in the rival playhouse, Drury Lane, in effect making Sheridan manager of the theatre. In the light of our knowledge of his later life, it is harder to understand why Sheridan accepted. He had a deeply equivocal attitude to theatres and actors and was incorrigibly unbusinesslike. It is one of the saddest ironies of theatre history that shortly after taking on the management of Drury Lane in 1776 – and immediately producing two masterpieces – Sheridan almost ceased to write plays or to make theatre his driving interest (it had to remain his business but there was at least as much harassment as enjoyment in his Drury Lane commitment). When in 1780 he took a step which placed politics at the centre of his life, entering the House of Commons as Member of Parliament for Stafford, he is on record as saying that it was the happiest moment of his life. With the exception of the operatic tragedy, *Pizarro* (in any case an adaptation from Kotzebue), there were to be no more plays from the once-fertile pen.

The early death of Goldsmith allowed no time for what might have been a fascinating and, one would hope, creative rivalry to develop between the two Irishmen. What we see instead is Sheridan following rather closely in Goldsmith's footsteps, most obviously in his general attitude to what comedy in the theatre ought to be. They shared a distaste for the sentimental comedy in vogue in the 1770s. Goldsmith conducted a campaign against the 'miserable hybrid', attacking it in his prose works and providing a rival comic genre, as he considered it, in his plays. Sheridan benefited from the enthusiastic reception given to *She Stoops to Conquer* which created a climate friendly to his own spirited, ironic comic genius. It was natural, then, for him to continue the attack on the sentimental genre, as he amusingly did in his second prologue to *The Rivals*.

The situation was more complex, however, than their satirising might suggest. Both Sheridan and Goldsmith were ambivalent in their attitude to sentiment. Sheridan evidently revelled in the opportunities it gave him to poke fun at its more extreme absurdities: had sentimental comedy not existed, he would almost have had to invent it, to give himself an inexhaustible topic of mirth (and something more complex, in his characterisation of the sentimentalising Joseph Surface). Their mockery of the genre did not inhibit either writer from including plenty of full-bodied sentiment on his own account. Goldsmith's sympathetic presentation of Mr Hardcastle, Sheridan's softness to Lady Teazle, show them moving with the current of the age rather than against it. Their apparently total dismissal of the new genre requires a closer look, as does the genre itself, for sentimental comedy was an interesting dramatic movement which expressed radical changes in eighteenth-century sensibility and social conscience. Playwrights as sensitive to audience response as Sheridan and Goldsmith could never have stood aloof from this crucial shift in public consciousness. Sheridan indeed showed how well he understood it by his skilful adaptation of Vanbrugh's *The Relapse* to the taste of his time (this adaptation is not all loss, any more than sentimental comedy represents a pure decline from the more acidly witty and bawdy comedies of the Restoration). For audiences of today the polemics on sentimental comedy have lost much of their force along with their topicality. Yet the attitudes which provoked the polemics remain highly germane to any discussion of Sheridan and Goldsmith. This will be the subject of chapter 4.

We may be tempted to regret the remarkable versatility which drew the two writers in so many directions, thus perhaps depriving the theatre of more masterpieces. There is another way of looking at it, however. It is just the variety of their mental life, the sense of vivacious, far-ranging interests and abilities that may help to answer one of the most difficult questions about their drama. How is it that plays in a way so emotionally and morally simple, in comparison with, say, the piercing ironies of the best Restoration comedy, have always been able to fascinate audiences and continue to do so in the theatre of our own time?

For it is a fact that of all the Irish playwrights who have poured their talents into the making of the English theatre, Sheridan and Goldsmith have probably come nearest to Shakespeare in their power of drawing whole-hearted, warm and interested responses from all sorts of mixed audiences in every period. Peter Davison comments that Sheridan's plays are in fact unique in their unbroken stage history of undisputed success.[1] They have inspired great actors and drawn appreciations from writers as subtle as Lamb, Hazlitt, Henry James (in his case, almost against his will). Charles Lamb, who had a glimpse of Sheridan's own actors before they left the scene for ever, paid the most memorable of all tributes to a single comedy: 'Amidst the mortifying circumstances attendant upon growing old, it is something to have seen *The School for Scandal* in its glory.'[2] The lines were gracefully adapted by Laurence Olivier, when he reflected on the hold *The School for Scandal* continued to exert on the affection and interest of actors (he had just been engaged in directing it): 'I am prepared to swear that whatever mortifying circumstances attend the life of the Theatre throughout the world, this play will never grow old.'[3] *She Stoops to Conquer*, *The Rivals* and *The Critic* have similarly drawn actors and directors of distinction – Tom Courtenay as Marlow; a glittering cast in the 1983 production of *The Rivals* at the National Theatre; Tom Stoppard brilliantly directing *The Critic* at the same theatre in 1985.

Yet these plays, so acceptable to the modern theatre, were very firmly rooted in the theatre of their time, as will be shown in more detail in the course of chapter 3. Sheridan and Goldsmith wrote for stages in some ways harder to imagine now than Shakespeare's more distant one. It is in some ways easier for us to appreciate Shakespeare's theatre – open to the sky and relying largely on natural light – than Covent Garden or Drury Lane in the 1770s. Their relatively modern appearance – roofed building, proscenium, scenery and so on – may well cause us to underestimate the chasm that exists between that stage and ours. Used as we are to brilliant lighting, how hard for us to think ourselves into a theatre as big as Drury Lane in 1777 which was yet lit entirely by candles and oil floats. Again, we seldom if ever experience the sort of audience participation all eighteenth-century theatre-goers took for granted; those moments before and after the play when an actor would step forward and talk to them directly about any subject the playwright wanted to air, usually also appealing for a favourable judgement on his play. It is not easy for us to assess the effect on audiences of these prologues and epilogues, often written by theatrical or literary celebrities on behalf of the author, like Dr Johnson's prologue to *The Good Natur'd Man*. It is as if Iris Murdoch or Peter Hall could be expected to launch the latest new play at the NT or the Barbican with a swift run-down on points of interest and a plea for an unprejudiced hearing.

Goldsmith and Sheridan wrote with the special conditions of their theatre very precisely in mind; the stage requirements, the talents of particular actors, and the interests of the audience. They quoted from contemporary literature and theatre, made all kinds of topical allusions and allowed themselves in-jokes that need footnotes for anyone unfamiliar with eighteenth-century stage history. Sheridan has an orgy of such jokes in *The Critic*, as when Puff, played by Tom King, uses the real names of the actors performing the play in 1779 to illustrate his powers of hype. It was a comic crescendo such as cannot quite be reproduced today when the sly list culminated in compliments to the speaker himself 'it is not in the power of language to do justice to Mr King!'.

The period feeling is so strong in these comedies that even in today's theatre, where it is almost second nature to set classics in some time other than their own, *She Stoops to Conquer* or *The School for Scandal* are seldom given such treatment but commonly retain their eighteenth-century look. Perhaps we are still in that phase defined by Shaw in which 'obsolete costumes and manners' positively add to the attraction of a play.[4] Or perhaps there is some pressure from the realism that is part of the comedy (a realism noted by Laurence Olivier and an important element, to which we will return). It might also be thought difficult to transfer to some other period the moral and aesthetic climate surrounding the Julias and Sir Olivers and Hardcastles.

Yet of course the plays have succeeded in soaring out of their environment and becoming a self-contained world in which anyone can feel at home. They provide a telling illustration of the paradox that in order to be universal it is first necessary to be intensely parochial. How was this done, what is there in these comedies to account for their admission into the modern repertoire as undisputed classics? Because they are so gloriously comic? No doubt of that – but what else? For there is something else; to do with irony and satire as well as farce, with feeling as well as fun, with morality and serious behaviour as well as intrigues and amusing complications. This is the sphere which can cause critical problems or discomfort even for some who admire the comic genius of both playwrights.

With its emphasis on rationality, uplifting sentiment and decorum the ethos in the plays can often seem more remote from modern taste than that in Shakespeare's comedies. The benevolent optimism that prevails may strike an alien note. We are more sceptical today about happy endings, more prone to demand a dose of realism mixed with them. How can we take without discomfort so pious a curtain speech as Julia's at the end of *The Rivals*, so complete a resolution of warring elements as in *She Stoops to Conquer*? Still more difficult, can we attribute any kind of seriousness to plays which (or so it might seem) ignore the darker side of life, omit the deeper notes struck in Shakespeare's comedies, famously in *Love's Labour's Lost*, with its reminders of death and the need for professing lovers to encounter the reality of life in hospitals? What too of the missing political dimension? This is not just a question of the severe eighteenth-century censorship which gagged all playwrights. On Sheridan's part, at least, the avoidance of political issues was a matter of deliberate choice (rather strange, we might think, in one who so immersed himself in politics). Some would add to this list of absences a lack of serious sociological satire, of the sharpness, even bitterness of a Wycherley or a Molière. For audiences reared on black comedy and farce far more outrageous and 'low' than the eighteenth-century theatre could have begun to conceive, there might seem something bland and insipid in the comedy of Goldsmith and Sheridan; one modern critic does indeed find *The Rivals* 'too inoffensive and vanilla-flavoured, too given to playing safe'.[5]

But is it really true that there is no sense of life's complexities and densities in the comedies of Goldsmith and Sheridan, that they offer only a witty and delightfully comic surface? The word 'surface' might give us pause, for Sheridan uses it himself in a pointed way in *The School for Scandal*, through the name of the two so unlike brothers, Charles and Joseph, drawing attention to something deep in his comedy, we might say at its heart. It is something that does indeed hold serious interest for moderns, is one of the great preoccupations of the modern stage; no less than the whole business of projecting personae; performing, as a function not just of the theatre but of life. It is the realm of masks and faces – of double selves – that is displayed with such comic élan in the dual personality of Marlow in *She Stoops to Conquer*, Captain Absolute in *The Rivals*, and, supremely, in the brothers who complement each other so neatly in *The School for Scandal*.

We have to bear in mind, of course, that the recurrence of masking motifs in these plays owes much to dramatic tradition. Disguises, pretences, mimicry are obviously the perennial stuff of comedy and were constantly used by Shakespeare, the Restoration playwrights, *commedia dell'arte*, Marivaux; all at one time or another models for Sheridan and Goldsmith. Some critics take a sternly censorious line on this, equating the use of conventional material with lack of originality. Both *The School for Scandal* and *The Rivals*, according to Marvin Mudrick, are no more than 'miscellanies of stagey, actable situations incorporating sentimental and stock-comic types'.[6] Critics less overtly hostile may still often be found agreeing that Goldsmith and Sheridan are recyclers of conventional material rather than innovative and original playwrights. *The School for Scandal* has been seen as 'an act of literary nostalgia',[7] *She Stoops to Conquer* summed up (by Hazlitt) as delightful and 'delicately managed' but somehow only a caricature, not a 'genuine comedy'.[8]

But there is an opposite viewpoint – in the theatre, at least, a majority one – which sees the two playwrights as far more than skilful imitators and adaptors. To those who carry incidents and lines from the plays in their heads as we carry Shakespeare's ('I can bear witness to that'; 'Lady Teazle, by all that's damnable!'), Sheridan and Goldsmith are indisputably originals, comic geniuses of the first order. Into the conventions they took over, and borrowing was indeed rife, they infused a fresh personal quality that results in the creation of an utterly new and distinctive dramatic world. The 'other' self as they represent it on their stages may be an amusing mask in an ancient theatrical tradition (Roman comedy, Italian *commedia*). But it can also hint at depths beneath and be adjusted with agile ease to allow the realistic lineaments of 'ordinary' eighteenth-century people to emerge.

For along with the bravura theatricalism – always drawing attention to itself with a great sense of fun – there are believable characters with feelings that require to be taken seriously. The nature of these feelings is often too simple or (inescapable word) sentimental for modern critics. Take, for instance, the attachment between Sir Anthony Absolute and his son, which underlies the comical bluster of the one and the cool wit of the other. In a good production this relationship can be found affecting and funny, all in one. It was so in the 1983 production at the National Theatre when Michael Hordern's Sir Anthony let his human need for closeness to his son glimmer through his tantrums. But this kind of revelation is apt to elude critics on the look-out for more complex or sophisticated motivation – or those for whom the conventional aspects of the characters drown out their human notes. For Hazlitt, Sir Anthony and Captain Absolute were the 'sterling characters' of the play. He did not underestimate the comical, conventional aspects but he could see real characters there too; one of them 'tetchy, positive, impatient, overbearing, but warm and generous'. For a modern critic over-preoccupied with 'types' and 'humours', however, the humanity in that portrait thins down to a figment; Sir Anthony is no more than 'Sheridan's rendering of a Jonsonian humour after the manner of Restoration playwrights'.[9]

Both Goldsmith and Sheridan present a special problem to criticism: how to appreciate with modern rigour plays which seem to defy or elude analysis by being so open, candid and straightforward. I suggested earlier that at least one aspect of the comedy offers itself for the kind of discussion that comes easily nowadays. This is its use of a playfully self-conscious theatricalism to express shifts and divisions in personality (the dual personae of Kate Hardcastle and the rest) and to draw attention to game playing as a process in which actors, audience and playwrights are equally involved. We are in home country here, with Oscar Wilde and a stream of modern plays about projecting the self through performance just round the corner. But still, there is the difficulty of connecting the theatrical sophistication (which we like to think of as modern) with the seemingly unsophisticated, or at least unmodern, benevolent morality which sets the plays' tone and dictates the happy endings. An extra problem for linguistically-oriented critics is the florid prose often used by the characters at their most serious. This tends to alienate the modern ear, though probably more in reading than in the theatre, where clever actors can do wonders with it as Fiona Shaw did with Julia's more sanctimonious speeches in the NT production of *The Rivals*.

Some of the disparaging commentary on the 'second-hand' and 'second-rate' quality of Sheridan's and, to a lesser extent, Goldsmith's comedy stems from an over-literary approach, a seeming unfamiliarity with the plays in performance (it is hard to believe that Marvin Mudrick, so cutting on Sheridan's 'stage tricks', had ever seen the plays on stage). But judgements more firmly based on theatre experience also tend to be remarkably divergent and contradictory, from the earliest to those of recent years. Even admirers cannot agree on what constitute the chief virtues – or failings – of the work. For one modern critic *The Rivals* has 'little apparent value'; another finds more in it but is still puzzled by the success of a piece which 'lacks real moral seriousness or high aesthetic design'.[10] One critic of *The School for Scandal* finds it strong in the invention of comic situations but weaker in wit, another asserts: 'It is generally acknowledged that Sheridan's plays succeed on account of their witty dialogue and in spite of their dramatic action'.[11] Henry James was torn in opposite directions, shrinking from the 'coarseness and harshness' of the back-biting scenes but announcing that 'for real intellectual effort, the literary atmosphere and the tone of society, there has long been nothing like *The School for Scandal*'.[12] Some praise the naturalness of Goldsmith while for Horace Walpole the worst thing about the characters in *She Stoops to Conquer* was that not one of them 'says a sentence that is natural' (he admitted that the situations forced him to laugh).[13] Few have felt able to take the robust position of Dr Johnson, who pronounced that the great end of comedy was 'making an audience merry'.

The idiosyncratic, contradictory nature of the critical responses over two centuries says something about the force coiled up in these seemingly harmless, uncontroversial comedies. Disagreement is one kind of tribute. There is also, of course, another kind; the devoted attention paid by modern editors such as Cecil Price and Arthur Friedman, by biographers like John Ginger and by the various critics who in the last few years have brought a sympathetic as well as sharp assessment to the plays. Yet it remains true that criticism has on the whole found the classical status of these comedies surprisingly difficult to account for.

One undeniable source of their power, their wit, is not always accorded quite its proper weight. Even Shaw, who defended Wilde's comedy against patronising references, chose, in discussing *The School for Scandal*, to focus not on wit but on morals. It was impossible to see the play, he affirmed, 'without beginning to moralise'. This has been the reaction of many critics. Of course the morality in the comedies of both Goldsmith and Sheridan raises interesting questions which we may find as stimulating as Shaw did (though Charles Lamb thought them irrelevant). Wit, however, is the yeast that lifts the moral matter into a new dimension. Lamb saw *The School for Scandal* as offering a respite from dull reality, 'two or three brief hours, well won from the world'.[14] And with the wit goes a quality not always found in conjunction: humour. Goldsmith's delight in his 'booby', Tony Lumpkin, Sheridan's ability to sympathise with both the Teazles; these are aspects of a humorous understanding which warms and softens the harder play of the wit. The writers' amused tolerance for the frailties they mock is an element in the appeal of their plays, as so often in classical comedy, from Aristophanes on.

Finally, we must return to the crucial paradox already touched on; the transformation by Goldsmith and Sheridan of utterly conventional material into something as fresh as paint and full of life's variety. Highly mannered, strongly oriented toward absurdity and farce as they are, their comedies also give us a real world, with a recognisable society, and convincing psychology. Faulkland writhing to hear of Julia's good health in his absence – 'Oh! d–n'd, d–n'd levity!' – is amusing through exaggeration of a trait that could be taken seriously with a slight change of emphasis (a clever production can get both effects). Tony Lumpkin's repeated 'I can bear witness to that' is an exhilarating comic chant which also expresses character, and makes sly comment on the way a fabrication like Mrs Hardcastle's story of the stolen jewels can acquire an uncomfortable independence of its begetter.

How was this transformation worked? The truth to life which audiences, if not all critics, have sensed in the plays, reflects feelings the playwrights were able to draw out of their own lives, including areas non-artists might have preferred to leave dark. Goldsmith projected something of his privileged but uneasy situation as an Irish member of Dr Johnson's circle through the divided, intermittently awkward Marlow. The Surface brothers divide between them opposing characteristics – improvident generosity/calculating deviousness – which Sheridan's contemporaries saw as features of his own nature. The playwrights' willingness to reveal the authorial self, however obliquely, helps to raise the emotional level of the comedy and give it the most important kind of seriousness; the attempt to be truthful.

It also matters, of course, that the personality revealed through its dramatis personae should be interesting and well-endowed. Such things as cadences, rhythms, literary allusions, ironies, pointed arguments, tell us that in these comedies we are in the best of company. In their light and airy way they remind us, without ever trying to do so, that the playwrights were admired members of the most intellectually sophisticated and cultivated circles of their day. Goldsmith was an intimate of Dr Johnson and the distinguished members of his Club, while Sheridan mixed with a dazzling cross-section of talented society from early youth – and in his turn joined the Johnson circle when elected to the Literary Club.

The achievement of Goldsmith and Sheridan was to infuse their unusually varied and stimulating experience of the worldly world with intensely personal, vulnerable feeling. They wrote close to the events of their own lives and succeeded in creating out of the conventions open to them comic forms that not only crystallised key preoccupations of the day but poignantly expressed their own personalities and inmost emotional drives. In the next chapter the lives will be viewed in relation to the plays.

2
The Lives and the Plays

To begin with Goldsmith. Like much in his life, the records of his date and place of birth are somewhat hazy. He was probably born in 1730, in Pallas, a village in County Westmeath, Ireland. His father was a country clergyman, prototype for the idealised Dr Primrose in *The Vicar of Wakefield*. Goldsmith had in high degree what Lady Gregory was later to call the 'incorrigible' Irish genius for myth-making. So, the village of Lissoy, where the family moved soon after his birth, became 'Sweet Auburn, loveliest village of the plain' of *The Deserted Village*, while the splendid joke at the centre of *She Stoops to Conquer* may have grown (at least in part) from an adventure said to have befallen Goldsmith as a youth. Walking in the country, where he had been noticed taking an interest in fine houses ('Gentlemen's' seats), he enquired at Ardagh for 'the best house in town' and was directed to the best 'gentleman's' house which he took for the inn he had really wanted. After behaving in a very free and easy way, calling for wine and the next morning, his bill, he learned that his host was no inn-keeper but an old acquaintance of his father's. The fact that there was a theatrical source for *She Stoops to Conquer* in Isaac Bickerstaffe's musical play, *Love in a Village*, does not exclude the possibility that an early embarrassment of the kind described provided some of the psychic drive that can be sensed behind the bizarre yet theatrically convincing situation in the play. It is typical of Goldsmith that he should turn such experiences (this one would have been especially mortifying for an adolescent) into comedy for everyone to laugh at. As Tom Davis points out,[1] Goldsmith with equal intensity idealised and strove hard to get away from the place of his childhood. After entering Trinity College, Dublin, in

1745, he set his sights elsewhere, making efforts at one time to study law in London, then to emigrate to America (twice) before being admitted to Edinburgh University to study medicine in 1752. Restless always, he left Edinburgh without a degree, having 'seen all that this country can exhibit in the medical way' and went to sit at the feet of eminent professors in Paris. He spent another couple of years travelling in Europe where he lived rough, sometimes supporting himself by playing the flute or by engaging in 'University disputations for a fee (He disputed his way through Europe, said Boswell).

There seems to have been little he observed in all his diverse experiences which he did not use as a writer. This included himself, the 'philosophic vagabond'. He faced the fact of his ugliness as he called it: smallpox had added its disfiguring marks to an irregular, puckish sort of face, with the prominent mouth – noticeable even in Reynolds' sympathetic portrait – which John Ginger aptly describes as 'wide, deflected at the corners, undershot, the full lips jutting forward like nose and temples'.[2] He admitted whimsically, in his deliciously playful letters to friends and family, to traits of character – like procrastination and excessive fondness for fine clothes – which added to the difficulties of being poor. He suffered from speech difficulties too; an uncouth or at least awkward delivery, highlighted by an Irish brogue which he apparently kept throughout his London days. He was a convivial soul, a lively conversationalist 'Who wrote like an angel, and talk'd like poor Poll', as Garrick famously put it. Characteristically, Goldsmith made creative use of this handicap, projecting it into the free dimension of comedy through the half-fluent, half-maladroit Marlow in *She Stoops to Conquer*.

Some of Goldsmith's awkwardness may have been due to his sense of being alien, an Irish fish out of water among the English (and, worse, the Scots). There is a world of self-understanding in his casual comment on Edinburgh social life: 'I shew'd my Talent and acquired the name of the facetious Irish man' (*L*, 18).[3] He wrote from Edinburgh to his uncle, the Reverend Thomas Contarine, that he had 'left behind in Ireland Every thing I think worth possessing, friends that I love and a society that pleasd while it instructed' (*L*, 5). He loved it, of course, as a dream place, one to be lived in through memory rather than in reality. Ginger suggests that his failure to return, even when he had the means, and when his mother, from whom he had long been estranged, was old, blind and ill, made for a sense of guilt that was subtly disseminated in the imagined relationship between a spoilt son and a doting but insensitive mother in *She Stoops to Conquer*. As with everything he experienced, he observed and meditated on his nostalgia. 'Unaccountable fondness for country, this maladie du Pays, as the French call it', he said, in a letter written after he had settled firmly in England. He could rehearse his reasons for not going back to Ireland ('perhaps there's more wit and learning among the Irish? Oh Lord! No!') but still: 'If I go to the opera where Signora Columba pours out all the mazes of melody; I sit and sigh for Lishoy fireside, and Johnny Armstrong's last good night from Peggy Golden.' Flamstead Hill was a 'magnificent prospect' but: 'I had rather be placed on the little mount before Lishoy gate, and take in, to me, the most pleasing horizon in nature' (*L*, pp. 28–30). The feeling for an idealised home place, a pastoral scene, enters strongly into the benign atmosphere Goldsmith creates in his best-loved play; loved perhaps just because it does, for all its fun and satire, so consistently strike that emotional note.

Goldsmith's curiosity about people was boundless; perhaps it was another reason for his being drawn to medicine in his youth. He evidently relished being Doctor Goldsmith (though he dropped the title in later life when questions arose about his formal possession of a degree). He practised for a time among very poor patients during his poverty-stricken early years in London. There is something pleasing about the thought of Goldsmith, like Chekhov, bringing the hard experience acquired as a doctor into the sympathetic ambience of his comedy.

After settling in London in 1756, Goldsmith earned a living as best he could – doctor, usher in a boys' school, apothecary's assistant, proof-reader. Rumour used to have it, based no doubt on his convincing descriptions of strolling players (as in *The Vicar of Wakefield*) that he had once been an actor. He certainly had a great sense of play, and might have done anything to keep afloat in the early years. But later his attitude to the acting profession was equivocal (like Dr Johnson's and, indeed, Sheridan's). He dissuaded his nephew from going on the stage because it was 'an abominable resource which neither became a man of honour, nor a man of sense'. This admittedly, was in 1771, when his Covent Garden experience might have implanted a few prejudices against theatre people.

Goldsmith was soon drawn into the Grub Street world. Producing articles and histories for the publisher John Newbery remained a much-needed regular source of income, even in the days of his fame. Journalism was the starting point for a leap into his true vocation as writer. His regular articles for *The Monthly Review*; his amusing letters from an imaginary Chinaman learning the odd ways of the English (The 'Chinese Letters' published in Newbery's *Public Ledger*, 1760–1, and later collected under the title *The Citizen of the World*); critical discourses like *Enquiry into The Present State of Polite Learning in Europe* (1759); these first put him on the map of letters. In 1764 his long poem, *The Traveller or a Prospect of Society*, brought him wider renown and admittance to the literary circle that revolved around the Grand Cham, Samuel Johnson. The Irish 'jester', the term he angrily used about the way he had been seen at the Duke of Hamilton's house (*L*, 17), became a founder-member of Johnson's Club (later the Literary Club) and an intimate of Johnson, Reynolds, Burke and the other distinguished people who made up England's foremost intellectual circle. He had an enormous success in 1766 with *The Vicar of Wakefield*, the novel which enabled Dr Johnson to save him from the bailiffs. As Boswell recounts Johnson's story, the Doctor had received a (not unusual) plea for help from Goldsmith to which he responded first by sending a guinea and then going to his lodging, where he found his friend virtually a prisoner; he had been arrested by his landlady for arrears of rent. Boswell (not sympathetic to Goldsmith but a good verbatim recorder) noted Johnson's ironic observations as well as his sympathy. The guinea had already been spent on a bottle of claret which stood open on the table, along with a glass: Johnson took the precaution of replacing the cork before enquiring what Goldsmith had in the way of marketable material. The manuscript was produced: 'I looked into it, and saw its merit; told the landlady I should soon return, and having gone to a bookseller, sold it for sixty pounds.' Goldsmith was enabled to pay his rent which he did, noted Dr Johnson 'not without rating his landlady in a high tone for having used him so ill' (*B*, 140). Here was another real-life episode loaded with a mixture of the absurd and the mortifying which Goldsmith was soon to adapt for projection on to the comic stage.

Goldsmith had to struggle hard to get his plays produced. It did not help his chances that he had been severely critical of current theatre practices in his *Present State of Polite Learning*, unmistakably targeting Garrick's management at Drury Lane. He deplored the theatre managers' habit of shunning new plays (to cut costs by avoiding the author's 'third night' benefit) and instead, resurrecting the 'lumber' of the past. Managers, he said, loved stage pomp more than dramatic quality, relied too heavily on Shakespeare and always put the actor first; the 'histrionic daemon' dominated the theatre. If an author did succeed in getting his new play accepted it would have a hard time of it, be 'tried in the manager's fire, strained through a license, suffer from repeated corrections'. It was unlikely, he concluded, that any writer of value would turn to the stage 'when he must at once flatter an actor and please an audience'.

Garrick cannot but have taken this ill. When *The Good Natur'd Man* was offered to him (Goldsmith was at work on it through 1766 into 1767) he could scarcely refuse to consider the first play of so eminent a writer (and intimate of Johnson's, who was pressing for acceptance) but he made matters as awkward as he could, insisting on submitting the script for an opinion from the undistinguished playwright and Poet Laureate, William Whitehead. Goldsmith later told Colman that he had angrily refused this 'tribunal'. After considerable friction, negotiations with Garrick failed and Goldsmith offered the play to the rival management at Covent Garden. George Colman, who had only just taken over as manager there, accepted it (without consulting his co-patentees, an action which resulted in their bringing a law suit against him) and *The Good Natur'd Man* was performed at Covent Garden on 29 January 1768, with a prologue written by Goldsmith's powerful supporter, Dr Johnson. It fell far short of the success Goldsmith had enjoyed in literature; partly, it would have to be said, because he had not yet fully mastered the stage art – and partly because he offended the audience's taste with the droll scene in Act III when Honeywood tries to pass off the bailiffs as his friends. The scene proved too 'low' for the first-night audience and had to be withdrawn. Probably other episodes, like that of the helplessly drunk butler, caused similar, if less drastic, tremors. Goldsmith did reasonably well financially – the play ran for nine nights – but did not make his fortune. He must also have been mortified by the runaway success of the play Garrick chose to produce rather than his: Hugh Kelly's *False Delicacy*.

The Good Natur'd Man is a play written very close to the author's life. It announces itself at the start as the story of a young man beset by debts and bailiffs, the quintessential Goldsmith situation. Looming in the background is the figure of the wise and influential uncle who has devised a plan to correct his nephew's feckless 'good nature'. He is severe in his judgement of Honeywood's folly but recognises that 'we must touch his weaknesses with a delicate hand. There are some faults so nearly allied to excellence, that we can scarce weed out the vice without eradicating the virtue.' Similar comments on the interweaving of faults and virtues in Goldsmith's own character were made by Dr Johnson. Goldsmith, he said 'referred everything to vanity; his virtues, and his vices too, were from that motive' (*B*, 366). In a moving tribute after Goldsmith's death he did not close his eyes to the warts in the portrait: Goldsmith 'had raised money and squandered it, by every artifice of acquisition and folly of expense'. 'But', said Johnson, 'let not his frailties be remembered; he was a very great man.' It is tempting to think of Dr Johnson as a prototype for the stern but benevolent Sir William. He stood in a not dissimilar, avuncular relation to Goldsmith as the older to the younger Honeywood; was similarly authoritative and esteemed, severe in moral judgement but strong in support. Boswell thought Goldsmith modelled himself on Johnson, tried to be more like him: perhaps some of this respectful attitude is reflected in Honeywood's readiness to accept so contritely Sir William's thunderous rebukes at the end of the play.

Goldsmith put more of his personality than his improvidence under the dramatic lens in *The Good Natur'd Man*. Honeywood's character is above all a puzzle. This was also how Goldsmith appeared to his friends. Even those most responsive to his genius found him a 'singular character', a mass of contradictions; quixotically generous whenever he had money but always in debt; an easy writer and eager conversationalist who was strangely maladroit in conversation; proud, especially of his calling, but also prone to play the fool. Reynolds, his close friend, thought his wish to be liked was so strong that he sometimes abandoned his 'respectable character as a writer' in order to bring himself on to a level where simple people could feel themselves his equal and be gratified.[4] Boswell characteristically commented: 'If it indeed was his intention to appear absurd in company, he was often very successful' (*B*, 139). There seemed to be agreement that he was envious, wanted always to shine yet would risk mortification by plunging into a conversation 'carelessly' without knowing how he was to get out again.

Dr Johnson's circle, with its emphasis on sense and proper reserve, its sprinkling of fine gentlemen with urbane English manners (and its worldly Scottish reporter) was not altogether the easiest context for an Irish writer and scholar who enjoyed letting his fancy play and thoughts stream out. His uninhibited candour tended to be seen as at best 'diverting simplicity', at worst as vanity that insisted on playing to an audience. When Boswell defended Goldsmith with a patronising 'For my part, I like well to hear honest Goldsmith talk away carelessly' Johnson replied with a severity worthy of Sir William Honeywood: 'Why yes, Sir; but he should not like to hear himself' (*B*, 240). Dr Johnson, however, saw more deeply into the nature of his fellow writer. He acutely observed, for instance, that Goldsmith was 'not a social man. He never exchanged mind with you'. This put the vexed gregariousness in a new perspective, as does Goldsmith's own comment that he always got the better when he argued alone: it suggests a habit of conducting mental arguments that would make it natural for him to turn to dramatic dialogue. John Ginger sees him as a compulsive day-dreamer and fantasist, mentally acting out the experiences of others when they caught his fancy and sometimes striking observers as over-reacting in the process.

So acute an observer as Goldsmith could not have failed to realise that his puzzling character was a topic for discussion among his friends. He makes it his own topic to some extent in both his plays. Some of the traits Johnson and the rest identified – the desire to shine, conversational gaucherie and enviousness – may sometimes have been their misreading of Goldsmith's Irish irony, which was often directed against himself in a playful, comically exaggerated way: one or two tall tales of his supposed insatiable desire for compliments suggest this. Boswell recognised the Irish element with customary condescension: Goldsmith had 'a more than common share of that hurry of ideas, which we often find in his countrymen, and which sometimes produces a laughable

confusion in expressing them'. Or, as A. N. Jeffares more under-
standingly puts it: 'Like most Irishmen he abhorred a conversational vacuum. If there was nothing else for the company to laugh
at he would laugh at himself.'[5]

Goldsmith's Irishness found its full release in his second play,
She Stoops to Conquer, written after he had enjoyed another
literary success with his narrative poem of Irish life, *The Deserted
Village* (1770). This must have been a boost to the confidence
dinted by his first theatre experience. Perhaps he was encouraged
too by the mixed success enjoyed by the sentimental comedies
which he thought of as queering his pitch. He returned to his
assault on the stage, as usual desperate for money and hoping for
better financial returns from theatre than literature had provided.
Yet again, he had a struggle to get his play accepted. Colman was
still doubtful about Goldsmith's theatrical abilities and his propen-
sity to the 'low'. Goldsmith wrote to him in January 1773, urging
him to come to a decision on the new play, offering to make any
changes Colman required 'without arguing about them'; finally
begging, 'For God's sake take the play and let us make the best of
it, and let me have the same measure at least which you have given
as bad plays as mine' (*L*, 116–17). Garrick, to whom he also sent
his script (though on second thoughts retrieving it) was evasive,
though he supported Goldsmith with a prologue. Strong persuasion – 'nay, a kind of force' – from Dr Johnson was necessary
before Colman, now a member of the Club, accepted the play. He
remained pessimistic about its prospects right up to the first night
(even then, when it was clearly a success, demoralising the anxious
author by making too much of an isolated hiss). The play was
known as 'The Mistakes of a Night' until the day before the first
performance when Goldsmith sent to the theatre (along with the
prologue for Mrs Bulkley, playing Kate) the brilliant new title by
which it was forever after known. *She Stoops to Conquer* had its
first performance at Covent Garden on 15 March 1773.

The play was a success in every way; it made Goldsmith money
though not enough – would anything have been? – to clear him of
debt. He wrote no more plays, only a last poem, *Retaliation*
(published posthumously in 1774). Had he lived, he would surely
have been in demand where previously he had struggled (he never
quite forgave Colman for his lack of faith, enjoying a mild revenge
by keeping him on tenterhooks as to whether he would mention

the matter in his preface to the published play). Garrick, with whom his relationship had become amiable, pleased him by wanting to revive *The Good Natur'd Man*. He looked forward to making changes in it, on his own initiative this time; he would create a new character and drop Lofty, a part he had decided 'does not do'. In the same month (December 1773) he promised Garrick a new comedy, to be ready 'in a season or two at farthest': 'I fancy I will make it a fine thing' (*L*, 127). Alas, before that season came round, Goldsmith had died, on 4 April 1774. With sad irony, the author of 'The Mistakes of a Night' died through a kind of mistake (insisting on being his own doctor and treating his illness with a medicine which apparently worsened it). A note of farce, some critics have observed, played its part to the end: but Goldsmith's death affected his friends painfully. Burke burst into tears, even Boswell, so often critical of the 'jester's' ways, paid him fitting tribute, and Johnson provided an epitaph which highlighted Goldsmith's astonishing versatility: 'Nullum quod tetigit non ornavit.'

Turning now to Sheridan, we find that he too used the material of his life in his comedy with engaging frankness, while also concealing it behind bravura comic masks. He performed an agile balancing act, like the Harlequins who played such an influential role on the eighteenth-century stage. Irishness was another strand in that imagination. Richard Brinsley Sheridan was born in Dublin, probably in 1751, son of the actor Thomas Sheridan and Frances Sheridan, novelist and playwright, on whose writings her son was to draw for his own plays. He was also, in less tangible ways, deeply influenced by his father. Thomas Sheridan for some time managed the Smock Alley Theatre in Dublin, intermittently fleeing from the tensions of that situation, including riots of almost unbelievable ferocity, on the lines of the worst kind of football hooliganism today. In 1754 he came to Covent Garden to act under John Rich's management and then changed to a second career as a voice teacher and writer on educational theory and practice. He also compiled a dictionary, became a friend of Dr Johnson and lost the friendship when he was awarded a government pension (having been one of those instrumental in obtaining Johnson's). The Doctor's concern that an actor had been put on the same level as himself ('Then I had better give up mine') expressed that disdain for acting as a profession already observed in Goldsmith. Johnson later added a kinder personal comment: he always made exceptions for individuals, as notably for Garrick.

Thomas Sheridan's son was aware from boyhood of the precarious standing of his family. When the Sheridans left Dublin for France in 1764, in flight from creditors, Richard was not taken abroad with them, but remained at Harrow School. It was the second time he had been separated from his parents (on the first occasion he had been left in Dublin, with the other children, in the care of relatives and then a foster mother). As a pupil at Harrow, entirely cut off from his immediate family, he evidently suffered some heartache. His letters to his uncle in London, requesting money to buy mourning clothes when his mother died abroad in 1766, are affecting documents. He seems to have been ill-provided for financially, hardly ever heard from his father and was altogether a deprived child. He also learned from the attitudes of his fellow schoolboys how low in the social scale the son of a 'player' was. His school years must in some ways have been as bitter to him as those Dickens endured on a humbler level when torn from childhood to work in the loathed blacking factory. His boyhood experiences could not have left Sheridan unmarked: it is a feature of his comedy that we do get glimpses into a more complex world of feeling, under the smooth comic surface.

On leaving school, Sheridan was reunited with his remaining family, joining them at Bath, where in 1770 his father launched an Academy of Oratory, collaborating with a well-known musician, Thomas Linley, on the 'Attic Entertainments' which publicised the scheme. Richard's love for Linley's daughter, Elizabeth, already celebrated at sixteen for her beauty and fine singing voice, developed through a series of spectacularly romantic episodes. The events around her courtship by an elderly man, who settled money on her despite her refusal to marry him, had already attracted theatrical mythologising: Elizabeth was the heroine of Samuel Foote's play, *The Maid of Bath*, before she became Sheridan's. When she resolved to escape the attentions of another importunate suitor, Mathews by name, Sheridan gallantly escorted her to France, where she briefly took refuge in a convent (an episode reflected in *The Duenna*). Sheridan had acted altruistically but was in love: the convent receded and the couple married, illegally, as they were both minors. Their romance retained its exciting secrecy when he brought her back to England (the habit of secrecy, says Sheridan's biographer, Madeleine Bingham, remained an important feature of Sheridan's character). He was obliged to fight two duels with the persecuting Mathews, in the second of which he was seriously injured – though not quite as catastrophically as the high-coloured newspaper reports of the affair made out.

The ease with which rumour took hold, facts were distorted and characters slandered, evidently came home to Sheridan with great force at this time. He said, in his light-hearted way, that he was reading the news sheets to find out whether he was alive or dead; but the joking cannot have expressed the whole of his feeling. He really had been near death at the hands of a quite unscrupulous opponent, he was in trouble with his father (always easily irritated, like his theatrical reflection, Sir Anthony Absolute); and he was oppressed by the opposition of both families to his marriage with Elizabeth Linley. That the experience was in fact traumatic is suggested by the way it continually reappears in his plays; duels, elopements, slander and journalistic exaggerations are the 'matter' on which he works his comic alchemy.

After a period of some months' separation decreed by Thomas Sheridan, who thought marital connection with musicians socially lowering, the Linleys capitulated (Thomas Sheridan remained hostile), and in 1773 the young lovers were finally legally married and set up house in London. Elizabeth could have supported them both with her singing but Richard forbade it as demeaning to them both, a decision approved by Dr Johnson: 'Would not a gentleman be disgraced by having his wife singing publicly for hire?' (*B*, 310). Ironically, the upshot of this quixotic decision was Sheridan's own move away from law, which his father had wished for him, into the socially dubious zone, first as playwright and then manager. Later, when he deployed his clever oratory in the House of Commons, he was liable to be reminded, as he had been at Harrow, that he was, after all, an outsider, more truly at home among actors than in the heart of the English élite. In a celebrated snub, Pitt commented on a speech Sheridan had made by praising his abilities – the pleasing effusions of his fancy, his dramatic turns, and his epigrammatic allusions – then sneering at them: if they were only reserved for the proper stage, they would no doubt ensure the plaudits of his audience.[6] Despite the brilliant social successes he enjoyed – his amours and friendships with duchesses and the like – Sheridan always remained something of the Irish outsider, as Goldsmith had to some extent been in Dr Johnson's circle. It is no accident that his comedies so often celebrate the exploits of dashing adventurers who win their way against odds, with the aid of their quick wits, histrionic abilities and powers of persuasion.

Sheridan had much less of a struggle than Goldsmith to break into the theatre. It welcomed him with open arms, as his letter to his father-in-law suggests, with its casual comment: 'There will be a comedy of mine in rehearsal at Covent Garden within a few days.' Goldsmith had undoubtedly paved the way with *She Stoops to Conquer*; its success must have convinced everyone, including the manager, Mr Harris, who had asked Sheridan for a play, that new work should be tried, perhaps especially when written by Irishmen. There were opportunities for Sheridan to see Goldsmith's play and it is clear from his own writings that he was well acquainted with it, as with Goldsmith's views on theatre: he tended to echo them, as will be seen.

The Rivals was the work of an inexperienced writer of 23 who had done little more in the literary line than write occasional verse and collaborate with his friend, Halhed, on a juvenile piece of verse translation, *The Love Epistles of Aristaenetus* (published in 1771) and a burlesque, *Ixion*. When *The Rivals* opened at Covent Garden on 17 January 1775 it had a mixed reception, due partly to erratic performance (the actor playing Sir Lucius O'Trigger was outrageously drunk) but also to some obvious faults in the writing: the play was too long and there were crudities, including expressions too rough for the audience at Covent Garden. They were naturally offended by Lee's woefully inebriated performance as Sir Lucius but they also looked askance at Sheridan's 'derogatory' characterisation of his Irish spitfire (in this first version of the play he was more murderous and lecherous). The *Morning Chronicle* deplored the slight cast on 'our brave and worthy neighbours' (on the other side of St George's Channel). Were those responsible for the unlucky casting of Mr Lee, which exacerbated the fault, possessed by an evil spirit – or was it a deliberate assault against 'the whole Irish nation'?. The play was also found dull in places; according to the *Public Ledger* it 'lulled several of the middle gallery spectators into a profound SLEEP'. Sheridan was not cast down. He took advantage of the customary nine nights' grace allowed a new play to withdraw his apprentice piece and revise it, working at great speed, with the coolness and effectiveness of a Jack Absolute. When the play was shown again, with a new prologue, written for 'the tenth night', the *Morning Chronicle* commended the improvements: reduction of excessive length, removal of certain 'objectionable and heavy scenes' and refined performances. Laurence Clinch redeemed the character who had given so much offence in a much softened version of Sir Lucius O'Trigger. The reviewer patronisingly pronounced that with more experience the playwright could be expected to produce 'a very capital play'.[7]

The tone of that last remark expresses the confidence in their own judgement felt by audience and reviewers alike. Sheridan did not fail to take note of the power they had to make or mar; they had helped him on this occasion to write a better play but there would be no gainsaying their verdict had it been unfavourable to his revised version. He kept the lesson in mind throughout his theatrical career.

His ability to write at great speed was demonstrated again that year. After *The Rivals* in January, he dashed off the lively farce, *St Patrick's Day: or The Scheming Lieutenant* and advanced in November to his amazing triumph with *The Duenna*, the piece which, as Cecil Price says, 'did more to establish Sheridan in the theatre than any of his other achievements'.[8] *St Patrick's Day* was performed on 2 May 1775 for the benefit night of Clinch: the merry afterpiece was a thank-offering to the actor who had restored Sir Lucius to popular favour. Its slight plot, crammed with ingenious tricks and disguisings, both draws on comic tradition and, as *The Rivals* had done, reveals something of Sheridan's more private preoccupations. Irishness is very much to the fore. The play opens with Lieutenant O'Connor dispensing money to his men on St Patrick's Day and the British soldiers anticipating the Irish toast they will drink: 'His honour, St Patrick, and strong beer for ever.' It ends with Justice Credulous forced to accept the profession and nationality of the young man who has snatched his daughter from under his nose:

Just: You're an Irishman and an officer, ar'n't you?
Lieut.: I am, and proud of both.
Just: The two things in the world I hate most – So mark me – Forswear your Country, and quit the Army – and I'll receive you as my son in law.

(II, iv, 197)

O'Connor indignantly refuses – 'if you were not the father of your Daughter there, I'd pull your nose' – and Credulous submits, persuaded by the Doctor, who assures him that the Lieutenant is in the right.

Sheridan more than made amends here for any unwitting slight he had put upon his nation in the characterisation of Sir Lucius O'Trigger. The plot of *St Patrick's Day* once again turns on the outwitting of the older generation and the winning of a 'tricking little baggage' by a spirited young man with a gift for mimicry and self-disguising. Sheridan seems to be trying how many variations he can play on the theme close to his heart. The key of farce is maintained but there are some moments in this lightweight piece suggestive of another Irish trait, the mixing of comedy with a more melancholy, musical strain, as in Dr Rosy's elegiac refrain: 'Flowers fade'. Written as a farcical afterpiece and received (with approval) as no more than that, yet *St Patrick's Day* casts its own small light on Sheridan's sensibility, especially his enjoyment of artfulness and his pride in his Irishness.

The Duenna was a more radical variation, a move into the collaborative world of music drama. Musicality of a kind had been apparent in Sheridan's plays from the start: cadence, rhythm, refrain gave his dialogue a musical emphasis which no actor (then or now) could afford to ignore. But *The Duenna* breaks out into real song. The musical family into which Sheridan had married was now seen to be a treasure trove to him. His wife (who wrote out the libretto) could give valuable advice on the singing roles; his father-in-law, Thomas Linley, provided him with settings and tunes and took over the musical direction at Covent Garden for the occasion, and young Tom, his brother-in-law, the leader of the Drury Lane orchestra, took charge of the score and provided new music for it. Sometimes the words came first, sometimes the tunes; old airs were adapted and new ones written; all this before the composers knew what the opera was to be about. Thomas Linley disapproved of the higgledy-piggledy method: 'I think he ought first to have finishd his Opera with the Songs he intends to introduce in it and have got it entirely new set: no Musician can set a Song properly unless he understands the Character and knows the Performer who is to exhibit it.'[9] Nevertheless he and his son poured out music to suit Sheridan's darting fancy: the combination of their melodic fluency with his mordant wit made *The Duenna* a refreshingly sweet-sour mix. It had a particular appeal for audiences at a time when the theatre was rather awkwardly divided between sentiment and heartier comedy.

The Duenna was performed at Covent Garden on 21 November 1775 and was an instant success, making Sheridan in abundance the money he so badly needed, since, as his father-in-law said, 'he will not be prevailed upon to let his wife sing'. *The Duenna* was as much admired for its spirited plot and witty dialogue as for its music. One reviewer saw it as rescuing the stage from the melancholy madness 'into which Cumberland and his sentimental compeers has lulled it'; all were agreed, despite occasional reservations (on excessive length, for instance), that it was a tonic and hugely entertaining. A little later, still higher praise was bestowed. For Hazlitt *The Duenna* was 'a perfect work of art' and Byron thought it far superior to 'that St Giles's lampoon, *The Beggar's Opera*'.

Posterity has not endorsed that extravagant claim, though *The Duenna* continues to amuse on revival and there have been triumphant new versions, such as Prokofiev's opera of the 1920s, performed to great acclaim at the Wexford Festival in 1989. The dramatic values will be examined later: here we may note that *The Duenna*, under the layers of impersonality imposed by the stylisation of comic opera and farce, keeps close, like the earlier plays, to the key events in Sheridan's own love story. It must have been amusing for Elizabeth, working with him on the libretto, to see her adventure taking comic shape in the melodious Louisa's strategies for freedom or in Donna Clara's flight to a Spanish convent, then away to love and marriage: 'For happier scenes I fly this darksome grove/ To saints a prison, but a tomb to love.' Louisa's duping of her tyrannical father was so close to home, James Morwood suggests,[10] that it could account for Sheridan wishing to keep his father-in-law in the dark about the plot of his opera. There is also a vein of more general satire, especially against religious hypocrisy. Sheridan's Whig sentiments can be faintly discerned here and there (he was to be a strong supporter of the French Revolution). In one jovially sardonic scene (III.v), the friars of St Anthony are presented at their drink, like Charles Surface's boon companions, toasting the ladies ('the blue-ey'd nun of St Catherine's').

To Garrick, on the point of retirement and seeking a successor to run Drury Lane, Sheridan must have seemed likely to fill the bill, despite his youth. He had displayed in *The Duenna* a real grasp of theatre possibilities, recognising, for instance, just how to use the special talents of individual actors. Garrick sold his half share in the theatre in 1776 to Sheridan and his partners (Thomas Linley and James Ford), Sheridan taking on the daunting task of business and artistic manager. Thomas Sheridan was to have been the 'acting manager' but his son's proviso that he should not also perform caused a rift – and delayed the appointment for a couple of years. Richard's old dislike of being seen as the 'player's son' seems to have been stronger than his wish for good relations with his father. It was a hint at the will to become an insider which was to be dominant in his parliamentary years. In the first flush of managerial excitement, however, he put considerable effort into his 'outsider's' task, as can be seen from the detailed memoranda he kept. Ironically, from one who was to use the theatre's money in a spectacularly loose way, there is much advice on small economies like saving candle ends.

Sheridan took advantage of his power over the repertoire to bring Restoration comedies (suitably trimmed) on to the Drury Lane stage. He announced his theatrical precedents, as it were, with the play which opened his first managerial season on 24 February 1777, *A Trip to Scarborough*. Somewhat to the disappointment of his audience this turned out to be not new Sheridan but old Vanbrugh, with a slightly new look. Sheridan's adaptation of *The Relapse* was the kind of exercise Garrick had been obliged to practise; tailoring the bawdy, sharply satirical comedies of a more plain-spoken age to the refined and squeamish sensibility of his own. Garrick had emasculated Wycherley in cleaning up *The Country Wife* (as *The Country Girl*) and Sheridan is said (on rather flimsy hearsay) to have admitted to spoiling Vanbrugh's play. The dramatic values of his adaptation will be considered later. As an exercise, it undoubtedly had value for him, testing his ability to strike the right note for his demanding audience. He succeeded in this, for after the initial disappointment they took to the adaptation: as a stage piece, it was preferred to the original for many years.

One of the changes he made hints at the strength of his family feeling and perhaps at some early nostalgia for the life outside London which he had enjoyed in his courting days. Unlike the scene of golden memory, Bath, which had figured so vividly on his stage, Scarborough never takes shape as a real place. Yet the title reminds us of his family with its clear echo from his mother's play (*A Journey to Bath*). And the provincial setting tunes with Sheridan's gentling of the characters and their language which robbed the seasoned rakes and belles of some of the hard power they enjoyed in Vanbrugh's London ambience (to which most of them rush with relief from the despised country).

Probably, as Arnold Hare suggests,[11] the rewriting of Vanbrugh's text was important to Sheridan as a preparation for his next play. If so, the exercise was well worthwhile, for the next play was his masterpiece. *The School for Scandal* opened at Drury Lane on 8 May 1777, with a famously accomplished cast, and to a storm of applause: the ecstatic response to the falling of the screen in the fourth act made a noise that terrified a passerby into thinking the theatre was about to fall down. The play was instantly recognised as a supreme work of theatre: almost everything about it seemed dazzlingly right. Stories told about it suggest a wish to see it almost as a magical event which had sprung from Sheridan's imagination at white heat, forcing the incorrigible procrastinator to write at top speed and the top of his bent. Best known is the story of how the fourth act was written in only one day, the under-prompter receiving single sheets as Sheridan finished them, then running between the house and the theatre 'like a pendulum' to deliver them to Hopkins the prompter for copying – just in time for the actors to learn their parts. Neatly, the story ends with Sheridan expressing relief on his own behalf and that of the sorely tried Mr Hopkins by scribbling on the manuscript ' – finis – Thank God! RBS – Amen! W. Hopkins'.

In fact Sheridan had been brooding for some time on the idea of the play and revised it rather obsessively. Many strands in the action relate closely to his private experience. One of the fragments from which it developed (known as 'The Slanderers') goes back to the time of the Bath duels and the rumours circulated about Richard and Elizabeth. Sheridan seems to have contemplated a darker treatment of the theme than he actually gave it. Still, it was a subject with special point for him.

In a more oblique form the play contains revelations about his own nature; no less deep for being cast in the genial comic form he had perfected. The two brothers, Charles and Joseph Surface, are contrasted with a sly irony which subtly insinuates the idea of their closeness. They are opposites who somehow belong together and strangely command almost equal sympathy. There was too much of both Charles and Joseph in Sheridan's own character for him to disown either. His father, who recognised the connections, thought it made writing the play an easy matter: 'Talk of the merit of Dick's comedy – there's nothing in it! He had but to dip the pencil in his own heart, and he'd find there the characters of both Joseph and Charles Surface.' The diagnosis was correct, though not the conclusion he drew from it. Everything known about Sheridan, notably in his period of theatre management, demonstrates that he had these warring strains in his personality; the reckless, candid, warm-hearted, dashingly charismatic Charles and the evasive, scheming, compromising, secretive Joseph. To express these serious contradictions so convincingly in blithe comic form was scarcely the easy matter his father took it for.

After the masterpiece there was a breathing space in which Sheridan master-minded an afterpiece, *The Camp*, performed on 15 October 1778. This was a lightweight topical entertainment inspired by an aristocratic romp in which the Duchess of Devonshire and friends put on military uniforms and held a 'Ladies' Mess' at the camp set up at Coxheath to prepare the Militia for possible invasion. French and Spanish troops were thought likely to land in support of the Americans in the War of Independence. The fanciful piece has interest chiefly as a work of collaboration which involved Tom Linley (who wrote the music) and Philip de Loutherbourg, the outstandingly original German designer who had joined Garrick's Drury Lane team in 1771 and had become a powerful force through his overall supervision of visual effects. His designs for *The Camp* provided the nucleus for the thin but visually exciting entertainment.

Sheridan's attitude to de Loutherbourg's triumphs must have been equivocal. It pleased him as manager: the designer's brilliance made a success for Drury Lane. But this success could be seen as a danger signal, a pointer to the possible takeover of the theatre by spectacle, an outcome hardly to be desired by a master of words. Sheridan dealt with that threat in the way that came naturally to his genius: he reduced it to absurdity in his next – and last – comedy, *The Critic*, presented at Drury Lane on 30 October 1779. It was a supremely good-natured satire, in which designer, actors and stage company took part in a great joke against the extravagances to which their various crafts might be subject. De

Loutherbourg himself was in charge of the designs for the orgy of scenic effects that eventually swallows up the play within the play: 'Spanish fleet destroyed by fire-ships . . . procession of all the English rivers and their tributaries.'

The Critic gives yet another demonstration of Sheridan's ability to transfer the material of his own life to the stage with ease and seeming artlessness. Harassments and minor oppressions like actors cutting lines or scenery going wrong are made elements in a totally liberating farce. The complex divisions of his mercurial personality were given a happy airing in this burlesque. Sheridan as author used Sheridan as theatre manager with the dexterity of a Surface brother or a Jack Absolute, calling attention to his double act with pointed in-jokes like the exchange between Sneer and Sir Fretful Plagiary (I.i) when Sneer questions Sir Fretful's decision to send the script of his new play to Covent Garden. Would it not have been better cast, he suggests, at Drury Lane? 'O lud! – no', Sir Fretful is alarmed: 'never send a play there while I live – harkee.' He whispers inaudibly in Sneer's ear, allowing the audience to savour in advance the sly joke which is to come in Sneer's straight-faced reply: '*Writes himself!* – I know he does – .'

The sly implication that a playwright who is also a manager has exceptionally good opportunities for plagiarism was a rather risky joke. Sheridan had been taxed with borrowing over-freely ever since the days when he took inspiration from his mother's fiction. But in his insouciant way he raises the bogie only to make nonsense of it. Is not Sir Fretful Plagiary on stage, to show us what the breed of plagiarists is really like? No more need be said: Sheridan can enjoy his joke and make his point in one. Evidently he did not care that Sneer's warning against sending scripts to Drury Lane might also remind some in his audience of the manager's dilatoriness in reading scripts (this created more serious problems after the death of Elizabeth, who read new plays conscientiously). All was grist to his ironic pen, not least his own frailties and peccadilloes.

This ability to put the different components of his character on public show in his comedies without apparent self-consciousness evidently connects with Sheridan's tendency to write at great – often enforced – speed, after initial procrastination. *The Critic* supplied another celebrated tale of his need to be pushed into a fast-writing situation. In order to get the last act of the play for which the actors were desperately waiting, Thomas King, who was playing Mr Puff, conspired with Linley to lock their author/ manager in a room at Drury Lane, well supplied with claret and sandwiches, and threaten to keep him there till the work was done. The strategy worked so well that supreme heights of comic brilliance were achieved in the dragooned act. Unprepared, improvising situations stimulated Sheridan, as he shows them stimulating the quick-witted personae in his plays. Unsurprisingly, *The Critic* charmed his audience in 1779 (although Sheridan had to do his usual pruning when it was found too long on the first night). That it has remained triumphant when revived in modern times is more remarkable, given the density of its topical reference. Even the absurd business of the Spanish invasion in Puff's play, which now looks only like stage fun, originally made sardonic reference to a topical issue, the public's renewed and wildly exaggerated fear of invasion in the months immediately preceding the staging of *The Critic* (and the theatre's response to their mood in the patriotic extravaganza, *The Prophecy; or Queen Elizabeth at Tilbury*, masterminded by Thomas King and performed June 1779). Sheridan was very ready to allow up-dating of the topicalities where this could be done: the acting text diverged quite drastically from his printed version during the play's run in his own lifetime.

Alas, after the fireworks of *The Critic*, Sheridan wrote no more comedies. Politics became the centre of his life. He entered the House of Commons as Member for Stafford in 1780, proceeding to win a second fame as rising Whig and friend of Fox; a holder of office (though only briefly); a dazzling orator in the House; a confidant, for a time, of the Prince Regent, who bestowed modest sinecures on him and his son, Tom. 'Insider' days, though always precarious, not least in his dependence on the increasingly strained finances of Drury Lane to support his political ambitions. In the cabals, plotting and strategies of politics he satisfied his taste for secret manoeuvres at the highest level, but he still found time to exercise control of Drury Lane. It was remote control on the whole, though interspersed with disconcertingly close scrutiny. Richard Wroughton, who succeeded Thomas King as sub-manager of the theatre in 1796, is quoted as rebuking Sheridan when he came once to a performance so drunk that he did not recognise the play as *The School for Scandal* and demanded the dismissal of the actor playing 'the old fellow' (Sir Peter Teazle). Wroughton sadly told him 'that we seldom see you here, and you never come but to find fault'. Drury Lane continued to have its triumphs, as how could it not with such actors as Sarah Siddons, John Philip Kemble, Dorothy Jordan, playing there. But its finances became hopelessly entangled with Sheridan's debts. Actors were not paid regularly: Mrs Siddons spoke of the 'drowning gulf' in which money owed to her was lost. She also noted, 'Still we go on'. Sheridan's charisma prevailed, along with the esteem won from his brilliance, his achievements, his faithful championing of the acting profession.

In whatever role he undertook, Sheridan needed to perform on a high level, with bold extravagance. Even at the height of his political career, he was able to find energy to inspire and direct a radical reconstruction of Drury Lane (1791–4). It involved the demolition of Christopher Wren's building and the creation by Henry Holland of a vastly enlarged and sumptuous new theatre on the old site. In this way alone Sheridan made his mark as manager of Drury Lane – though it proved an ephemeral memorial, for only a few years after the Holland building had been completed, in 1809 it was destroyed by fire. The news came to Sheridan in the House of Commons, when he displayed a heroic sangfroid. The House should not adjourn, he said, in reply to a sympathetic proposal to that effect, because the calamity 'was not of a nature worthy to interrupt their proceedings on so great a national question'. Still more heroic – and theatrical – was his famous retort a little later when surprise was expressed that he could calmly sit, with a drink, in the Piazza Coffee House, watching his theatre burn down: 'A man may surely take a glass of wine by his own fireside.'

It is hard not to see this bravura as acting, even if the part was one rooted in Sheridan's complicated personality. His underlying feelings cannot but have been darker. He was a man of sentiment as well as irony: when Elizabeth died in 1792 (having previously given birth to a child, not his) he found moving words to express his grief – and remorse for his neglect and faithlessness which had gradually impaired their idyll. These sombre notes in his private life were to be reflected, though distanced by rhetoric, in the last full-length play he wrote. Between 1779, the year of *The Critic*, and 1799, when *Pizarro* was produced, his contributions to Drury Lane as author had been limited to the occasional prologue or collaboration. He is credited with a share in the pantomime

Robinson Crusoe, described as 'highly inspired' by one theatre-goer, Edward Pigott, when he saw it in 1781, and in *The Glorious First of June*, a piece of flag-waving for a naval victory in 1794. But there was only to be one more substantial piece from his own hand and this was a tragedy, the first and last he attempted.

Pizarro (Drury Lane, 24 May 1799) has frequently been seen as just the kind of play Sheridan made fun of in *The Critic*; excessively high-toned, oozing with melodramatic incidents, depending to a great extent on grandiose spectacle and sadly without humour. It was an adaptation of *The Spaniards in Peru* by the German writer, Kotzebue, whose extravagantly romantic, rhetorical drama was enjoying a vogue. His *The Stranger* (in a translation refined by Sheridan) had already been seen at Drury Lane in 1798. Sheridan behaved like a good manager in making the adaptation available to his theatre. With his name attached to it as well as Kotzebue's, with the promise of spectacular scenery, with Kemble as the heroic Rolla, Mrs Siddons as Pizarro's mistress, the production was destined to be a winner. Sheridan had kept his sense of what the audience wanted. It was the age of revolution, the dawn of Romanticism, a time conducive to sympathy with heroic tales of brave Indians resisting invasion and oppression by cruel Spanish tyrants.

The play was also a serious expression of Sheridan's personal devotion to high romantic concepts of freedom and revolution. His choice of a fable (the word was in vogue among theatre reviewers of the time) tuned with his stance in politics as a Whig and staunch defender of the French Revolution. His most famous speech in the House of Commons was an emotional attack on colonial tyranny. When Sheridan followed Burke in the House of Commons in 1787 to make the case for impeaching Warren Hastings for maladministration as Governor-General of India, he focused especially on the pitiable situation of two Indian princesses, the Begums of Oude. They were, as he saw it, victims of Hastings' attempts to force repayment of huge sums of money owing to the beleagured East India Company by the Vizier of Oude. In Sheridan's hands the story shaped itself like a romantic melodrama. The Vizier was shown to have extorted treasure from his helpless mother and grandmother in order to repay his debt to the English, while in the background the chief villain, Warren Hastings, pulled the strings, contriving 'to harden the son's heart, to choke the struggling nature in his bosom'. The speech in the Commons lasted over five hours and caused a sensation, so much so that when Sheridan spoke in the trial of Hastings at Westminster Hall in June 1788, people competed to pay £5 for a ticket to hear him: it was like a theatrical occasion, booked out before opening.

Lewis Gibbs has commented that no one now is going to be carried away by Sheridan's account of the Begums' woes.[12] But his speech remains interesting as a massive statement in political form of beliefs that also form the ethical backbone of his plays. The emphases in the Warren Hastings speech connect very directly with the rhetoric of *Pizarro*. 'Is this the character of British justice?', Sheridan demands, and answers: 'No, I think even now I hear you calling me to turn from this vile libel, this base caricature . . . to the true majesty of justice here.' So, in *Pizarro*, Elvira calls on Pizarro to 'profane not the name of justice or thy country's cause', while pleas resound throughout the play for the tyrant to show mercy, above all to helpless young mothers like Cora. Links between the speech and the plays also extend back in time to earlier plays. Jack Durant has convincingly demonstrated[13] that the importance attached to filial piety throughout the Hastings speech ('Filial Love! the morality, the instinct, the sacrament of nature, a duty') is anticipated in the value set on Charles Surface's feeling for his surrogate father, Sir Oliver. Other values are replicated from play to speech; as, for instance, censure of deceit and hypocritical pretences of virtue. Durant points out that in some texts of the speech particular turns of phrase occur that are as appropriate to Joseph Surface as to Warren Hastings. The theatrical character was also given to the 'windings of mysterious hypocrisy and of artificial concealments' with which Hastings was charged and was equally 'ever fertile in expedients'. From the vehement patriotic tirades invoking freedom to the subtle investigations of the masks worn by ambitious men, Sheridan's speech of 1788 shows him still completely in touch with the playwright he had been – and was yet to be, if only in the last fling of a tragedy adapted from another man's.

Like Goldsmith, he spoke of writing another comedy, but in his case it was not premature death that prevented him. One of the saddest stories from the myth that formed around him in his lifetime tells how when he mentioned the possibility he was told by his hearer that he dared not do it, would be too afraid. 'What am I afraid of?' 'The author of *The School for Scandal.*' It was a shrewd if chilling diagnosis. *Pizarro* was a huge success; Sheridan had not mistaken his audiences' readiness for extravagant romanticism. But it was his last such triumph. He wrote no more and his life story became one of decline, with drink a plague and money troubles at their worst. After the fire of 1809 that destroyed his new Drury Lane, he suffered the humiliation of being barred from any further involvement in the theatre by Samuel Whitbread, in the past his sponsor: he would not fund the rebuilding if Sheridan kept any share in the theatre's business. Three years later Sheridan lost his parliamentary seat (he succeeded Fox at Westminster in 1806) and with it his immunity from arrest for debt. The last years of indigence, arrests and borrowing are painful to contemplate. He was not exactly alone, having married again in 1795 (the much younger Esther Ogle, daughter of the Dean of Winchester – a marriage right into the Establishment). And he had some family satisfactions, in his son, Tom, for instance. But he seems a lonely figure at the end, with friends falling away and theatrical pleasures long receded.

Sheridan died on 7 July 1816. At once the author of *The School for Scandal* reassumed his place in the esteem of the nation: he was accorded a funeral fitting his achievements and buried in Westminster Abbey. With his compatriot, Goldsmith, he achieved full insider status at the end.

3

The Plays in the Eighteenth-Century Theatre

The comedies of Goldsmith and Sheridan were partly shaped, like all actable plays, by the form and conventions of the stage for which they were written. Certain features of both writers' technique are clearly related to staging methods and acting conventions at Covent Garden and Drury Lane in the last quarter of the eighteenth century. Equally clearly the two placed their personal stamp on the theatrical conventions they took over.

A word is needed on the nature of the theatres themselves; Covent Garden, for which Goldsmith wrote exclusively, and Drury Lane, which became Sheridan's domain. They were the only theatres in London empowered by the Licensing Act of 1737 to present the drama of the spoken word, though Italian opera (and its English follow-up, ballad-opera), pantomimes and various ingenious forms of wordless farces flourished in theatres like the Haymarket and Little Haymarket. The popular, 'illegitimate' forms had a wider impact on the art of the legitimate theatre than is always recognised. They made their free way into the repertoire of the two patent houses as the farcical or harlequinade afterpieces which followed the main drama. Farce succeeding tragedy raised no eyebrows then as it did when Laurence Olivier presented his celebrated double bill of *Oedipus* and *The Critic* in 1945. Some of the mannerisms of the 'other' theatre seeped into the style of both Goldsmith and Sheridan. The latter in particular had a natural affinity with the art of the harlequinade (Garrick first came to notice playing Harlequin and was an accomplished mime). The masked, agile, endlessly inventive Harlequin, jumping through scenery, dodging enemies, displaying his skills in plots and masquerades, could be seen as an archetype for Sheridan's own ingenious, plotting heroes (or a reflection of himself, as is implied in the title of a modern critical study, *Harlequin Sheridan*).

In discussing such things as shape of stage, lighting, and acting conventions, what is said of one of the two patent houses can usually be taken to refer in a general way to the other. There were divergences but the two tended to keep abreast, watching and emulating each other's moves. When Goldsmith's first play was produced, Covent Garden (built in 1732) was the more modern of the two theatres but Garrick had done much to bring Drury Lane up to date, notably by installing a new lighting system which was ahead of Covent Garden's. At the time Sheridan took Drury Lane over, it had enjoyed a major refurbishment, with designs of great elegance and airiness by Robert Adam which made the house seem bigger, though as one reviewer noted, it was an illusion created by 'the ingenious Artists'. Sheridan himself, as we have seen, was responsible for more drastic changes when, in 1791, he had the old Wren building demolished and replaced by Henry Holland's much vaster edifice. The new Drury Lane housed between 3600 and 3900 spectators, compared with the 1800 of the former theatre. The stage 'accommodations' for this mammoth (completed in 1794) were described by the architect as 'upon a larger scale than any in Europe'. The proscenium arch was 43 feet wide and 38 feet high and the actors were at a far greater distance from their audience than in the old house: it has been calculated that they needed to project 100 feet, compared with 60 feet in the Adam theatre. To Sarah Siddons, the new theatre was a 'vast wilderness'. It called for performance styles on a correspondingly grand scale and one of its critics, Richard Cumberland, thought it destroyed the possibility of fine nuance in acting. The audience, he said, would cease to be 'hearers' of a text and become merely spectators to a show (*Memoirs*, 1806). In the usual leap-frogging way, Covent Garden enlarged to the fashionable new size in 1792. We need to be aware of these changes, in part because they help to establish the intimate scale of the earlier theatres for which Goldsmith wrote both his plays and Sheridan all but one of his; and also because it was for the 'Modern Drury' that Sheridan wrote *Pizarro*.

Perhaps the staging feature that would strike us most forcibly today, if we could be transported back to the first nights of *She Stoops to Conquer* at Covent Garden or *The School for Scandal* at

Drury Lane, would be the co-existence of a large forestage, making for a close, intimate relationship between actors and audience, and a proscenium stage, where an illusion of scenic realism could be created by means of painted wings and back-flats. The proscenium frame demanded above all pictures; framed scenes, insets, tableaux and the like. The move to the moralising tableaux of melodrama had begun, as can be seen in Richard Cumberland's play *The Note of Hand* (1772), which opens with an elaborate visual statement:

> A Gaming-House, Rivers is discovered asleep on a couch; dice boxes on the table, with candles nearly burnt out; the floor spread with cards, and his hat and sword lying upon it; the room in great disorder. Sunderland enters; and, after contemplating him some time, speaks: 'So, so! broad noon and your night just begun – what drudgery it is to be a gamester!'

Sheridan was completely the master of the proscenium effect. He created two of the most famous picture scenes in the history of comedy in *The School for Scandal*. Both occur in Act IV, making the act a mighty climax and watershed. In scene i he presents the audience with an elaborate picture which represents a room full of pictures: a 'frame within frame' effect. After the auction has been conducted in the 'picture room' (so called in the stage direction), there is a brief interlude, still in Charles Surface's house, in the more modest setting of the parlour. It was possibly played in front of the drop curtain which was customarily lowered – though usually only between acts – to allow scene changes to be conducted out of view. However, the audience was equally used to seeing flats slid along their grooves to effect changes of set. Overt artifice and realistic appearances co-existed easily in staging – as it does in the plays. Following the unassuming parlour episode, came another spectacular, large-scale picture in scene iii; the grand library, in the house of the other brother, Joseph Surface. The pointed juxtaposition of the brothers' rooms draws attention to the central importance in the play of the closeness as well as the contrast between the two (rather amusingly, the association of deceitful Joseph with books offended Shelley, who took it as a slight on literature).

The juggling with appearances that his stage demanded suited

Sheridan's interest in social façades and surfaces. His art thrived on a scenic convention that could combine a painted façade in a flat dimension (as for the picture gallery of IV.i) with solid theatrical properties like the actual pictures which probably hung on the wings, to take the illusion a step nearer verisimilitude. Possibly they were the same pictures that had been used in *The Rivals*, in Act III.iii, when Captain Absolute, waiting for his tricky meeting with Lydia under Mrs Malaprop's eye, 'Walks aside and seems engaged in looking at the pictures'. Sheridan enjoys drawing attention to the artful nature of the illusion by having his characters make play with it. In Act IV.i Charles and Careless construct additions to the set from objects on the stage, setting them against the painted scene, to stand out from the illusion and at the same time enhance it. Charles behaves like an actor, seizing on mundane pieces of furniture and turning them into 'properties'. An auctioneer's stand is provided for Careless by the 'old gouty chair of my Grandfather's' (appropriate because of its extended leg rest): the rolled-up parchment containing the family tree becomes the hammer to knock down the goods. The auction is set up, in fact, as a kind of theatre game; one that is being played in earnest, for Charles must have money and Mr Premium must be persuaded to buy his pictures.

The sparseness of furniture on this stage made up of wings and painted flats was no disadvantage to a playwright such as Sheridan. Quite the opposite: it allowed him to invest any objects he used with enormous significance. In the library set of scene iii the shelves of books are painted but there must be at least one real one, the volume Joseph snatches up when Sir Peter makes his inopportune appearance. A more acute observer than he might have wondered about the discrepancy between Joseph's profession of devotion to books ('the only things I am a coxcomb in') and his vandalish throwing away of the book he was supposedly engaged on when interrupted. One eighteenth-century actor playing Joseph turned his page down carefully before laying the book aside; an action in line with the neatness Joseph boasts of, but losing Sheridan's point about the holes that show from time to time in his carefully prepared surface.

A contemporary illustration (p. x) of the library scene shows a back wall painted to represent at one end a window giving on to a view of trees, but for most of its length lined to the ceiling with books:

this is the learned façade that so impresses Sir Peter. The illustration registers the moment when the screen has fallen, to reveal Lady Teazle. She is placed well back in the set behind the proscenium. The audience were thus given a good view of the stage picture: they could enjoy to the full the amusing tension building up round that mute piece of furniture that could tell so much if it could speak. The screen is a still point in a picture that is continually being recomposed around it as new visitors arrive and other hiding places are opened up. Sir Peter goes off into the 'closet' to listen in on Joseph's conversation with Charles, leaving the stage perhaps by a proscenium door or one artfully constructed in a scenic wing or simply through the wing, without concession to the realistic illusion (it was not till much later that the wings were regularly closed in so as to form the more realistic box set). Only when every opportunity for hiding, being hidden and overhearing has been exploited to the full, does the screen fall – at exactly the right moment, with Charles and Sir Peter on stage and Joseph re-entering in time to hear the fateful lines:

> 'Lady Teazle, by all that's wonderful!'
> 'Lady Teazle, by all that's damnable!'
>   (IV.iii.386)

The suspense gathering round the screen has a comical aspect which is well appreciated by Joseph, despite the precariousness of his situation. When Sir Peter admires the article, unaware whom it is hiding, Joseph responds with a double-edged remark which is clearly meant for his own amusement – and the audience's:

Sir Peter: . . . . you make even your screen a source of knowl-
                edge – hung, I perceive, with maps.
Surface: Oh yes – I find great use in that screen.
                                    (IV.iii.120)

Double entendres of this kind – very definitely meant not to be understood by the person to whom they are ostensibly addressed – found their natural home on the forestage. The illustration in the Frontispiece locates Charles Surface and Sir Peter Teazle in that area, watching the fall of the screen from a position remarkably close to the audience in the side boxes. This position, in front of the 'scenium', was the actors' favourite. It was by far the larger part of the whole acting area (30 feet wide and 20 feet deep in Garrick's Drury Lane): the 'scenic stage' behind was relatively shallow. The front boxes, with their galleries above, were only 25 feet from the front of the stage, while as the illustration shows, some boxes were right over the stage, adjacent to the proscenium doors. These doors (real, practical doors with a balcony above, also providing seating for the audience) were the actors' loved entrance and exit points. Throughout the later part of the eighteenth century a covert battle was going on to push the actors further back into the set, make them more completely part of the stage picture (the proscenium doors were even abolished for a time in the Holland reconstruction of Drury Lane).

The art of the aside, however, depended on the actors' use of the forestage: here they could play to their audience in a natural, easy way, making confidences or dropping ironical asides in the midst of the dialogue. Some actors overdid this intimate connection: Sheridan has a dig in Act II.ii of *The Critic* at 'the established mode of springing off with a glance at the pit'. But the counterpointing of aside or soliloquy with dialogue is a chief source of amusement – and interesting revelations – in his comedies and Goldsmith's.

The scenes from *The School for Scandal* just considered are rich in interplay of dialogue and aside or half-aside (as in Joseph's remark on the screen). It is a feast of the spoken word at its most easy and intimate, with throwaway remarks and covert jokes playing a descant to the rhetoric going on elsewhere. When Joseph holds the stage, this descant is at its most ironic. Like a comic Iago, he uses the aside to invite the audience into his plots and enjoy his sardonic view of his own and others' behaviour. When Sir Peter confesses that he dreads any frailty of Lady Teazle's being made public, Joseph is addressing the audience as much as his stage listener in his dry comment, 'No – you must never make it public'. Other more regular '*asides*' (so marked in the text) can be envisaged spoken out directly to the audience or treated as inner thought which the aside convention permits us to overhear. So, when Sir Peter reveals the financial generosity he intends to his young wife, Joseph at once imagines (correctly) the remorse of Lady Teazle behind the screen, and shares the thought with us: 'I wish it may not corrupt my pupil.' Told by Sir Peter that he does not want Lady Teazle to know of his generosity, Joseph ruefully reflects, 'Nor I – if I could help it'. In the first scene of Act IV, where Charles Surface holds the stage, significantly it is not he who is given the '*asides*' vantage point. He is up-stage, a public figure, conducting the auction with brio. It is his uncle, Sir Oliver, who keeps close to the audience, letting them into his state of mind and drolly expressing his dismay at the cavalier disposal of the family faces: 'Heaven deliver me! his famous uncle Richard for ten pounds!'; 'poor Deborah – a woman who set such value on herself!' He was evidently positioned on the forestage in such a way that he could easily take part in the auction while dropping his private sentiments *sotto voce*. His asides are a psychological necessity, like Joseph's. In a more benevolent style he too is playing a part and must have an outlet for the self that is suppressed. He can hardly contain his delight when Charles refuses to sell the portrait of the 'ill-looking little fellow over the settee'; his uncle has been good to him and 'egad, I'll keep his picture while I've a room to put it in'. Sir Oliver's double act becomes frenetic at this point; 'Mr Premium' tempts Charles with munificent offers – 'I'll give you as much for that as for all the rest' – and 'old Noll' revels in Charles's adamant refusals. Finally asides come so thick and fast, they threaten to break into the dialogue.

> *Charles*:   Don't tease me master broker, I tell you I'll not part with it – And there's an end on't.
> *Sir Oliver*:   (*Aside*) How like his father the dog is! (*Aloud*) Well, well, I have done; (*Aside*) I did not perceive it before but I think I never saw such a striking resemblance (*Aloud*) Here's a draft for your sum.
> (IV.i.114)

Sheridan showed this mastery of stage facilities from the start: his youthful first play, *The Rivals*, calls confidently for continual – and manageable – changes of interior and exterior sets. A remarkably full picture of the characters' life in Bath builds up as we move from North Parade to South Parade or King's Mead Fields, from Lydia's dressing room to Jack Absolute's lodgings or Bob Acres'. Characters bump into each other in the street, come and go at speed, give an impression of mobile, bustling life, indoors and out. The Drury Lane stage, with wings as well as doors for exits and entrances, made it possible to convey this flow of public and private activity without strain. It is harder for the modern proscenium theatre to capture that effect. However, the 1983 NT production in the Olivier Theatre did so by imaginative use of a stage which in its different way proved to have some of the eighteenth-century assets; notably an intimate relationship between auditorium and open stage, combined with the technical capacity (obviously far beyond old Drury Lane's) to create spectacular scenic effects. The Olivier Theatre simply became the city of Bath. Great scenic illusions of Georgian parades and crescents built up a panoramic view; actors came and went with equal ease on stage or through the friendly, fan-shaped auditorium, as if from one part of the city to another; domestic interiors took convincing, realistic shape within the modern version of de Loutherbourg's painted scene (an extra one was created to allow Michael Hordern's Sir Anthony to conduct his second confrontation with Jack (III.i) cosily over breakfast rather than in the impersonal spaces of the North Parade).

In this first play Sheridan also demonstrated his grasp of the 'asides' technique. Jack Absolute is at home anywhere on the stage but takes a good share of the forestage for the asides which keep the audience in touch with his quicksilver thinking. 'Gently, good tongue', he tells himself when he almost gives the game away to Mrs Malaprop in Act III.iii, by careless use of Beverley's name. He retrieves brilliantly, only to have his nerve tested again later in the scene, when Mrs Malaprop bursts in, announcing that she has overheard his conversation with Lydia. 'Oh, confound her vigilance', he says, *sotto voce*; and then, on realising she has misinterpreted what she heard: 'So – all's safe, I find.' The aside is already functioning here (as later with Joseph Surface) to help a plotting, deceiving character keep close to the audience's sympathies. Jack may need sympathy-gaining devices less than the colder-hearted plotter, Joseph Surface, but some he does need. So does Mrs Malaprop, whose eavesdropping might forfeit sympathy. She retains it with an aside in comic vein before she hides herself to spy on the young lovers: 'I'm impatient to know how the little huzzy deports herself.' Moral reservations tend to dissipate before malapropisms!

Command of the full range of stage techniques came more easily to Sheridan than to Goldsmith at the apprentice stage. *The Good*

Natur'd Man is not notable for its scenic effects; no especially memorable visual images are created and asides are rather conventionally used. It was not until he had found his true subject in *She Stoops to Conquer* that Goldsmith's handling of stage conventions acquired verve to equal Sheridan's. The crucial scenic requirement in the play was a house sufficiently like an inn for the person mistaking it as such to seem not too much of a fool. Goldsmith gave his scene designer one basic stipulation: the Hardcastle house should look 'old-fashioned'. He evidently considered it an important direction, for he repeats it (in his previous play his directions had been of the sparsest, 'Mr Croaker's house' and so on). The worn, out-of-date appearance of the house might go some way to suggest the style of a shabby country inn that had seen better days. Goldsmith made sure of the point by having Mrs Hardcastle complain within a minute of the play's opening that she has to live in an 'old rumbling mansion, that looks for all the world like an inn but that we never see company'.

He then ensures that the likeness of house and inn will be kept to the fore by switching at once in scene ii to the Three Pigeons, to reveal Tony Lumpkin sitting among 'several shabby fellows'; he is at the head of the table, placed 'a little higher than the rest'. The tableau – described with unusual fullness for Goldsmith – makes clear to the audience that the youth so awkward in the previous scene is here in his element. His mother saw her home as little better than an inn; he sees an inn as much better than his home. In acting as a link between the two places he emphasises their ambiguity. With such touches, scenic as well as verbal, Goldsmith builds up a sense of environment as something fluctuating and unstable. Mr Hardcastle's house, like the Three Pigeons, changes character according to who is looking at it; whether the owner himself, who loves everything old-fashioned, his wife who hates it, or the son who lives between the shabby house and the shabby inn and finds it easy to see one in terms of the other. The house is a chameleon, even before Tony performs his wicked alchemy. So the audience need not think Marlow too absurd for accepting the view ingeniously planted on him. When he and Hastings enter the Hardcastle house, they cannot but 'recognise' features Tony has misleadingly identified for them, including, no doubt, the 'large horns over the door' which supposedly denote the 'Buck's Head'. The 'antique, but creditable' appearance of the house strikes both travellers, in fact, as something familiar; the decline of a once superior residence: 'Having first ruined the master by good house-keeping, it at last comes to levy contributions as an inn.'

Goldsmith uses the full extent of his commodious stage in this play. He creates interesting scenic groupings, as when the revelations of Act V.iii conclude with Kate and Marlow retiring 'to the Back Scene', she 'tormenting' him as they go. Her teasing is in fun, but the stage picture gives us a fair idea of who is to be the controlling spirit in their marriage. Earlier in the same episode, Goldsmith may even have given a hint to Sheridan for his more famous screen scene. Kate directs her father and Marlow's to conceal themselves behind a screen so as to overhear the conversation with Marlow that will explain the mystifying discrepancies between her account of their relationship and his.

Goldsmith especially delights in the opportunities given by the forestage for ironic counterpointing or revelations of feeling. He brings each of his main characters forward to speak '*solus*' (a direction distinguishing more leisurely reflections from the quick aside). After Mrs Hardcastle's quarrelling exit with Tony in Act I, Mr Hardcastle remarks, 'Ay, there goes a pair that only spoil each other', then continues with a characteristic reflection on the rude manners of the age and his dislike of seeing his loved daughter, 'fond of gauze, and French frippery, as the best of them'. Kate is given her chance of the forestage as soon as her father exits, to express her mixed feelings about his account of Marlow: 'Sensible, good-natured; I like all that. But then reserved and sheepish, that's much against him.' Even in the crowded scene of the ale-house (I, ii) space is found for Tony Lumpkin to step forward, '*solus*', and confide in the audience that his motive for the trick he is playing on Marlow is to get his own back on his stepfather for 'calling me whelp, and hound, this half-year'.

Asides are so frequent on occasion as to form a second, *sub rosa* dialogue, amusingly responding to the main dialogue (which would be conducted in full voice, while the asides, on the fore-stage, could be *sotto voce*). As the plot revolves entirely round mistakes, the characters are all baffled at one time or another and one function of the asides is to bring this out. The two young men confide in the audience their satirical view of their pretentious 'landlord' – 'We shall soon hear of his mother being a Justice of Peace' – while the equally taken-aback Mr Hardcastle calls for sympathy from the audience at the cavalier treatment he is receiving from his guests: 'Their impudence confounds me.' Asides also allow for fuller revelations of character. Marlow in particular needs chances to raise audience sympathy for his odd, uncoordinated behaviour. The forestage allows him moments of honesty and distress, as when he braces himself to meet Miss Hardcastle in Act II – 'I have just been mortified enough in all conscience, and here comes something to complete my embarrassment' – or, at the end of their first, painfully formal interview, confides in the audience, 'This pretty smooth dialogue has done for me'. The asides punctuating the dialogues between Marlow and Kate (in her three different personae) keep the audience in touch with the fluctuating and complicated feelings of the two. We observe Marlow becoming less emotionally inhibited as his asides turn ever more frank and despairing. When, in her role as poor relation of the Hardcastles, Kate pretends to cry at his departure (IV.i), he pours out his new feeling to the audience: 'This is the first mark of tenderness I ever had from a modest woman, and it touches me.' While Kate is given the forestage to herself for another solo turn to express her sense of the importance of this same dialogue: 'I never knew half his merit till now. He shall not go, if I have power or art to detain him.'

In these ubiquitous asides Goldsmith is doing on a small scale what Eugene O'Neill was to do on a staggeringly large scale in his nine-act play of asides, *Strange Interlude*. Goldsmith was committed, of course, to a farcical plot which could not be too interrupted by the expression of inner feeling. That he makes as much room for this inner life as he does is a measure of his own interest in character. The shape of his theatre allowed him to keep a sense of naturalness and ease in the continual *sotto voce* of the forestage; an effect more difficult to achieve in large modern proscenium theatres. On some of the adaptable modern stages, however, the naturalness Goldsmith and Sheridan achieved with asides can still be captured; as productions of *She Stoops to Conquer* and *The Rivals* in the Olivier Theatre have shown.

Another feature of the eighteenth-century theatre which would strike us today, was the lighting. There was no separating chasm, as normally in a modern theatre, between a darkened auditorium and a brightly lit stage. As the whole theatre was lit by candles and oil floats, the lights remained on throughout, with actors and audiences 'under the same light', to use a phrase of W. B. Yeats, who hankered after just that kind of intimacy. This lighting would surely seem to us extremely inadequate for a theatre of such a size (especially if we were sitting in the furthest reaches of pit or boxes). By Sheridan's time, Garrick had introduced relatively sophisticated deployment of candle and oil lamp power to Drury Lane: the circular chandeliers over the stage had been removed and direct side-lighting provided by perpendicular candle battens behind the wings. This would have improved the general effect by removing glare but the concept of a steady lighting state remained; inevitably, for tinkering with such volatile lights was inhibited by the ever-present hazard of fire (as it was, both theatres burnt down within a few years of each other). The possibilities for selective, atmospheric lighting were therefore very limited.

These lighting arrangements exerted some pressure on writers to set plays indoors, if they wanted realistic effects; and realism in staging was on the increase. The most natural looking sets from this viewpoint would be those representing such places as the parlours of well-to-do homes, which would have been lit in actuality by domestic versions of the theatre candelabra. Comedy in the 1760s and 1770s, most obviously in its sentimental form, was moving toward a realistic portrayal of bourgeois domestic life, the life style its audience knew best. In the plays of writers such as Kelly and Cumberland the settings usually approximate to what the viewers in the more expensive seats would recognise as realistic; that is, candlelit rooms under a steady light. Cumberland's *The West Indian* begins in a merchant's counting house, moves from there to a drawing-room and thereafter shuttles among different domestic settings, all interior. *The Clandestine Marriage*, by Garrick and Colman, is set indoors except for one garden scene. With the manager of Covent Garden thus showing the way, it is no surprise to find Goldsmith's first play, *The Good Natur'd Man* (written for Colman's theatre), being set entirely indoors. His natural tendency was towards the outdoors and picaresque but he curbed it, setting his first four acts alternately in Young Honeywood's apartments and Croaker's house. Only in the last act did he move outside the domestic frame, to the less select environment of an inn. The scene is still an interior, however – and the inn is the superior kind, likely to have a well-lighted reception room for the benefit of good-class customers like Olivia and Leontine.

Inn settings seem to have been for the extraordinarily decorous and squeamish eighteenth-century audience a rough equivalent of the hotel setting in 1930s comedy; a compromise between select privacy and the dangerous public world where people of any class or type might walk in upon the high-life scene. Once Goldsmith had acquired confidence, he gave himself more freedom. The tone of the inn is decidedly lower in *She Stoops to Conquer* – and the play has a heartily bucolic outdoors scene into the bargain, the dread Crackskull Common, as Mrs Hardcastle believes, though in fact it is only her own garden. A stage illusion of darkness was required here, though Tony's vivid account of the night-terrors around them is a *tour de force* independent of scenic effect.

Sheridan was freer from the start with the scenic illusion. *The Rivals* opens in a street in Bath and continues to move out into the parades and crescents of the city. Opera had its own conventions, so it is nothing out of the way to find *The Duenna* beginning with a night scene in the streets of Seville, Lopez carrying a dark lantern and reflecting like Mozart's Leporello on the discomfort of being servant to an importunate lover. The account of the various sets used in the opera gives a fair idea of the backflats that were likely to be in regular use at Drury Lane: street scene, piazza, grand saloon, library (coming up again in *The School for Scandal*), garden and so on. *The Critic* simply takes the incongruity of candlelit daylight scenes for granted, starting with Mr and Mrs Dangle at breakfast before moving into the rehearsal sequence where every kind of theatrical illusion is to be happily brought low. *Pizarro*, as said, was written for a different theatre and also defies realistic illusion with its grandiose settings of temples and ravines. Only *The School for Scandal* keeps close to an illusion of realism, being set entirely indoors.

Returning now to the intimate relationship between stage and auditorium, we may see how this helped to make prologues and epilogues an obligatory element in plays. A seating capacity of around 1500 to 1800 might not seem so very small to us now, but numbers are misleading since spectators were squeezed into a space which nowadays would be licensed for only half that number. The close packing practised by Garrick or Colman had its obvious hazards and discomforts but helped to strengthen the sense of intimacy. Seating arrangements at Covent Garden and Drury Lane further accentuated it. Three tiers of boxes enclosed a pit which sloped down to the forestage: the audience 'papered the walls' as has been said.[1] We have already noted how close to the stage the side boxes could be.

The importance of the audience as an equal collaborator in the dramatic process is a point made continually in the prologues and epilogues which accompanied most plays (new ones as a matter of course). Basically, prologues pleaded for the audience's favour and epilogues hoped it had been won. As Garrick had announced from the stage when he became manager of Drury Lane in 1747 (in words written by Dr Johnson): 'The drama's laws the drama's patrons give/ For we that live to please must please to live.' The 'patrons' expected ingenuity and variety – entertainment, in fact – from these direct addresses which were usually spoken by actors with major roles in the play concerned, though sometimes by guest performers. Henry Woodward, who had no part in the play, spoke the prologue to *She Stoops to Conquer*. These 'framing' speeches could take the form of miniscule plays, like Garrick's epilogue to *The Clandestine Marriage*, which has eight characters, engaged in card games and discussions of Shakespeare and theatre matters ('What are your opr'as to Othello's roar/ Oh, he's an angel of a Blackamoor'). This was skittish: but though the audience liked a humorous approach, they were prepared to be seriously interested in the cultural or critical issues raised by a prologue, as in Cumberland's appeal to the audience to sympathise with the Irish character in his play, *The West Indian*. He was 'Sent by your sister kingdom to your shores/ Doom'd by religion's too severe command/ To fight for bread against his native land.' Sentimental comedy spawned many polemical prologues. Audiences would have enjoyed the double ironies implicit in the appearance of Tom King, a much-loved comedian, to speak Garrick's prologue to a quintessentially sentimental play, Kelly's *False Delicacy*. He pretends to be inveighing against the sentimental genre and does utter some home truths: 'For our fine piece, to let you into facts,/ Is quite a sermon – only preach'd in Acts.' But King, who had a major role, also courts favour, preparing the audience for the new kind of part he is about to delight his audience with: 'But even I Tom Fool, must shed some tears.'

The close, friendly, even conspiratorial, nod and wink connection with the audience which a prologue or epilogue allowed was the smiling aspect of a relationship which could be more severe and threatening. The audience had no compunction about hissing a performer's behaviour, private as well as professional: Mrs Siddons once had to defend herself from the stage against suspicion of mercenary behaviour. Such improvised moments obviously had a tremendous dramatic charge. Writers of prologues and epilogues often aimed to capture a similarly unscripted effect, so giving the actor a chance to show his mettle (actors receiving last-minute scripts from Goldsmith or Sheridan needed this in abundance).

Goldsmith characteristically exploited the idea of improvisation in both the epilogues he wrote for his plays. For the prologue to *The Good Natur'd Man*, he wisely relied on Dr Johnson to speak for him (apt casting, if Johnson was the prototype for stern but benign Sir William). Influential backing was important, as Goldsmith had been rather rude to the audience in his 'Chinese Letters', making his imaginary Chinaman describe noisy critics who needed to be taken down a peg or two. From his seat in the front of the pit, the area frequented by the wits, the Irish 'Chinaman' noted the hierarchical seating arrangements, with the poorest in the highest part of the house, and drily commented that distance from the stage did not affect the vociferousness of the 'masters of the ceremonies': those aloft had 'all the insolence of beggary in exaltation'. Dr Johnson's prologue took no such saturnine view but paid the audience the sort of compliments they were more used to. If anything, it was the author who was denigrated, being described first as the 'little bard', and then, on Goldsmith's objecting to the epithet, as 'our anxious bard', a no-doubt accurate if still rather lowering account.

Johnson's stately prologue drew a somewhat laboured parallel between voters at a political election who could be bribed and the Covent Garden audience who always expressed their true views. The playwright need not worry about his lack of 'ill persuading gold': 'But, confident of praise, if praise be due,/ Trusts, without fear, to merit, and to you.' This did what was required, nor could Goldsmith, writing the epilogue, afford to be any less conciliatory. He evidently found the requirement a nuisance – and characteristically made the nuisance of it his subject. His epilogue is about the theatre's demand for epilogues ('things can't go on without it') and the difficulty of finding writers for the task. There are good-humoured digs at the 'art of coaxing up the town' and at his own status as a medical doctor. One of his 'brother' doctors is imagined

complimenting Goldsmith in the act of declining his invitation –
'What, plant my thistle, sir, among his roses!' – while Colman, he
of the shaky faith in his new playwright, comes in for a share of the
sunny irony: 'Go, ask your manager – Who, me? Your pardon; /
Those things are not our fort at Covent-Garden.' And the miniscule drama ends with an up-beat vision of a would-be theatre-goer
unable to get a seat for a new play, gazing enviously at his 'simpering friends' in the pit, none of whom 'will budge to give him place'.
The actress entrusted with the epilogue, Mrs Bulkley (who played
Miss Richland) was given a good theatrical range, including a
travesty line of *King Lear* followed by a witty, dignified couplet
appealing for fair judgement:

> Blame where you must, be candid where you can,
> And be each critick the Good-natur'd Man.

Goldsmith's medical status (that doubtful quantity) was highlighted again by Garrick in his prologue for *She Stoops to Conquer*. The audience were urged to take the Doctor's potion, and so
cure comedy of her sickness (while also determining Goldsmith's
standing: 'Pronounce him *regular*, or dub him quack'). The epilogue again fell to Goldsmith, who had great trouble with it. The
choice he and Colman made from various draft versions was a
routine variation on Shakespeare's 'seven ages of man' speech,
scarcely very appropriate either to the dramatic situation or to the
character of Kate Hardcastle in whose person Mrs Bulkley delivered it. Critics have tended to wish that an alternative offered to
Goldsmith by Joseph Cradock had been preferred (spoken in the
character of Tony Lumpkin, it is a robust assertion of rustic
individualism).

One of Goldsmith's own discarded versions, however, has even
more interest, showing how naturally it came to him to turn little
upsets into good-humoured but sharp-edged comedy; and how he
yearned for music on his stage. His 'squabbling' epilogue was
inspired by a quarrel between Miss Catley, a singer whom he had
invited to perform an epilogue written for her by Murphy, and Mrs
Bulkley, who threatened to throw up her part unless the epilogue
were given to her, 'according to the custom of the theatre'.[2] She
won but not before Goldsmith had made a last attempt to include
some music by writing for actress and singer to deliver between

them a vivacious quarrel scene in which they invite the audience to judge their respective claims. The performers would have appeared in their own persons, Mrs Bulkley claiming, 'I've all the critics and the wits for me' but getting a dusty answer to her call for a show of hands: 'What, no return? I find too late, I fear, /That modern judges seldom enter here.' Miss Catley would have wooed the audience with patriotic ballads tuned to 'the bonny Scot' and the 'brave Irish lads'. Finally the two would have agreed to leave the poet 'un-epilogued', mocking his refusal to 'thrive by flattery', though 'he starves by wit'; a bold assertion of independence on Goldsmith's part.

Such was the personal charge Goldsmith brought to a bland convention of his theatre. Sheridan also expressed through these curtain speeches an aspect of his personality. His innate theatricalism showed itself in his first prologue, to *The Rivals*, when he cast his address to the audience in the form of a lively debate: two lawyers argued his case and promised the 'jury' that he would stand or fall by their judgement. Conventional sentiments, but exuberantly dramatised. In the prologue to the revised version, spoken on the make-or-break tenth night, he wisely avoided personal appeals, focusing instead on a topic of general interest and again producing a miniature drama. Though there was only one live actor – Mrs Bulkley (playing Julia) – she had company in the form of three effigies, representing Tragedy, Comedy and Sentimental Comedy. Pointing to each in turn, she invited the audience to join her in mocking the 'goddess of the woeful countenance', the Sentimental Muse. Goldsmith had given him the lead and Sheridan followed it up in gleefully histrionic style.

By the time of *The School for Scandal* Sheridan scarcely needed to propitiate his audience in advance. In fact both prologue and epilogue for that play were written by others, Garrick and Colman respectively: the first was spoken by Tom King as Sir Peter Teazle, the second by Frances Abington as Lady Teazle. Writers and speakers made up a glittering quartet of theatre luminaries who knew that in speaking for Sheridan they were backing a favourite. Sheridan used a prologue of his own for *Pizarro*; a curious choice, for there seems little connection between the play's lofty, tragic characters and the prancing 'cits' and 'white-rob'd misses' whom he sardonically portrays enjoying the 'suburb pleasures of a London May' in Hyde Park and 'rural Kensington'. As always, however, the emphasis is theatrical: it is his playful way of apologising for offering a 'Winter Drama', or tragedy, out of season. The evocation of Londoners at sport in a cold Maytime reminds the audience that spring can have its wintry side too. Perhaps too the comic sprightliness of the introduction was a subliminal reminder that the adaptor of Kotzebue was also the author of *The School for Scandal*.

The form a prologue or epilogue took could depend on which actor was chosen to speak it, as astute writers appreciated. An understanding of the actors' special abilities was an important asset for playwrights in this theatre which, as Goldsmith said, gave pride of place to the 'histrionic daemon'. Goldsmith, coming to the theatre as a literary man, had less control over his choice of actors than Sheridan. He was lucky with his first play to have an accomplished cast, some of whom played for him again in *She Stoops to Conquer* and may even have unwittingly supplied him with hints for that play. He certainly knew from vivacious Mrs Bulkley's performance as Miss Richland that she was capable of realising spirited heroines. Perhaps his creation of Kate Hardcastle owed something to the style of the actress. Mrs Bulkley in her turn was wise enough to recognise that Goldsmith gave her the opportunity to realise one of the most appealing heroines in English comedy. Other actors were less discerning, possibly infected by Colman's nervousness about the idiosyncratic nature of Goldsmith's comedy. Henry Woodward, who spoke the prologue to *She Stoops to Conquer*, had turned down the part of Tony Lumpkin, a decision he must surely have regretted immediately after the first night. Goldsmith was ready to seize on any special talents his actors had. He might not have managed to get music into the epilogue but Quick, as Tony Lumpkin, brought it into the play with the roistering song 'made upon this ale-house, The Three Pigeons'. He remained throughout someone liable to break into song, or at the very least, a whistle.

Sheridan inherited actors as well as much else from Goldsmith: several from the cast of *She Stoops to Conquer* took roles in *The Rivals* which called for similar characteristics. Once manager of Drury Lane, he acquired total control of casting, as of repertoire, and had chances to go much further than Goldsmith in one of their shared interests, the use of music in drama. *The Duenna* triumphantly demonstrated his ability to handle singers as well as actors.

He was also alert to the skills in mime and movement which flourished on the eighteenth-century stage. These show up comically in *The Critic*: actors absurdly exit on their knees, silently praying, or command the stage with portentous muteness, as in the sequence that culminates in Lord Burleigh's 'charged and majestic nod' (J. C. Trewin's phrase for Ralph Richardson's performance). The apparently effortless affinity between the actors and his characters was a much-remarked phenomenon. Charles Lamb, who had seen the tail-end of the original casting, thought that the part of Joseph Surface could never again be played so perfectly as by the first, John Palmer. He was, said Lamb, 'twice an actor in this exquisite part. He was playing to you all the while he was playing upon Sir Peter and his lady.' Sheridan did not write *for* his actors (his characters spring from a deeper source). But he used their particular attributes in a way that made audiences feel actor and part had always gone together. When Lady Teazle was played by Mrs Abington, an actress renowned for her special brand of seductive charm, Joseph's dangerous attempt on her, so out of keeping with his customary caution, may surely have seemed inevitable, as perhaps Sheridan intended.

Sheridan's easy mastery of the theatre situation, his familiarity with all branches of the theatrical art, from acting and design to administration and publicity, inevitably became his subject as well as his metier. Nothing so central to his private life could have failed to attract him as a playwright. In *The Critic* his satire had some specific targets; pretentious contemporary dramas like *The Spanish Armada* or individuals like Richard Cumberland, prototype for Sir Fretful Plagiary. But the reason for the play's enormous appeal, long after such allusions have ceased to be instantly recognisable, is its exuberant immersion in the fantastic business of theatre. We may miss particular literary or political points but it is enough to be taken up into this ironic – and affectionate – comic vision of the theatre at rehearsal, totally absorbed in itself.

Some of the in-jokes of the eighteenth century can carry over easily into the twentieth; the snide 'always late at that theatre' tends to draw laughs anywhere. Modern equivalents could no doubt be found for the acting styles satirised by Sheridan's actors (for they too had their chance to send up their profession). Bannister's Don Whiskerandos guyed the death scene of 'Gentleman' Smith in *Richard III*, as a modern comic might Anthony Sher's.

Sheridan's actors were required to keep the straightest of faces, while hearing themselves fulsomely praised by name for their performances, as in Mr Puff's illustration of his advertising skills:

> Mr. DODD was astonishingly great . . . That universal and judicious actor, Mr. PALMER, perhaps never appeared to more advantage than in the COLONEL, – but it is not in the power of language to do justice to Mr. KING!
>
> (I.ii.190)

The special beauty of this for Sheridan's audience was that the real Mr Dodd (Dangle) was listening to his own praise, and the real Mr King (Puff) praising himself. Sheridan does not forget the stage crew, giving them a chance to make their presence on stage really felt. Mr Hopkins, the long-suffering stage prompter, is addressed in his own person, respectfully. The scene shifters are given delectable chances to interrupt the action and do drastic damage to love scenes. The star of the show in the end, after all, is to be not an actor – not even the demented Tilburina nor the divinely mute Burleigh – but the scenery (strange anticipation of the magisterially mobile curtain which swept the actors about the stage in Lyubimov's 1980s *Hamlet*). De Loutherbourg, designer for *The Critic* in real life, becomes a character in the play when Mr Puff praises his abilities in his model advertisement: 'The miraculous power of Mr. DE LOUTHERBOURG's pencil is universally acknowledged!' Sheridan was laughing at himself in all this. His advertisements for Drury Lane were every bit as hyperbolical as Puff's – and it was he, after all, who underwrote de Loutherbourg's dominant role there. There may have been a sharp edge to his enjoyment of the stage joke when everything goes wrong, River Thames blunders ('hey! what the plague! you have got both your banks on one side') and the naïve author is left conducting the chaos hopefully. Sheridan gave the actor no detailed instructions at this point, saying only 'During this scene, Puff directs and applauds everything'. What new flights of comic improvisation occurred as the run went on, who can say? Sheridan would surely have been charmed by one such in the modern theatre: Laurence Olivier's Mr Puff, caught up on a piece of moving scenery, was carried up to the flies in the general débacle, still desperately trying to direct the scene which was swallowing him up.

Scenic effects are part of the joke in *The Critic* from the moment when Puff complacently prepares Dangle for a treat – 'Up curtain, and let us see what our painters have done for us' – and Tilbury Fort is revealed, with the two sentinels absurdly asleep beside the (no doubt) convincingly painted scene. In *Pizarro*, by contrast, scenery is taken very seriously indeed. Sheridan's stage directions, much fuller than in earlier plays, call for elaborate scenes to create darkly romantic atmosphere. Though following a scheme laid down by Kotzebue, he could not but have had his own theatre's capabilities in mind. De Loutherbourg had retired by now but design sketches of his were probably used[3] for the succession of astonishing spectacles. Spanish sets like the 'magnificent Pavilion near Pizarro's tent' contrast with the untamed Peruvian land-scapes; the 'wild retreat among stupendous Rocks' (III.i); the thick forest in 'a dreadful Storm' (V.i); the 'romantic part of the Recess among the Rocks' (V.iv) and the rocky place 'with a Tor-rent falling down the Precipice' (V.ii) where Rolla pulls up the tree forming a bridge across the torrent, after escaping across it with Cora's child in his arms. Peru was also allowed its own regal splendours, to match those of Spain – and to give the audience a spectacular scene change when the wild wood where Cora plays with her child (II.i) was replaced by the Temple of the Sun with all its 'magnificence of Peruvian idolatry'. The realisation of these exotic scenes (their atmospheric power frequently height-ened by accompanying music) was a major source of the play's popularity.

Another was the acting of the two stars, Sarah Siddons and John Philip Kemble. They were seasoned Shakespearian performers, highly skilled in the art of rhetoric. Mrs Siddons was famous for her deep, tragic tones and awe-inspiring stateliness (amusing stor-ies were told about her incongruous use of the tragic voice when making mundane enquiries in a shop about quality of goods). Sheridan knew he could rely on this powerful stage presence to carry the drama through its more extravagant moments; as when Elvira, thought to have been executed by her vengeful lover, Pizarro, makes a ghost-like appearance in a nun's habit, causing him to falter and lose his battle – and his life. The author of *The Critic* could scarcely have been unaware of the danger of bathos in the almost unremittingly high style the characters have to main-tain. Mrs Siddons and Kemble could be relied on to make their

lofty exchanges dramatically persuasive, as when they argue over
the morality of assassinating the tyrant:

> *Rolla*:   The God of Justice sanctifies no evil as a step to-
>   wards good. Great actions cannot be achieved by
>   wicked ends.
> *Elvira*:   Then, Peruvian! since thou do'st feel so coldly for
>   thy country's wrongs, this hand, tho' it revolt my
>   soul, shall strike the blow.
>
>   (IV.i.200)

Sheridan the satirist of *The Critic* of course co-existed with
Sheridan the orator who had roused public feeling against the
'tyranny' of Warren Hastings. In this vein it was easy for him to
adapt Kotzebue's throbbing rhetoric on behalf of the Peruvian
victims of Spanish tyranny. The ghost of his difficult, talented
father, who never succeeded in establishing himself at Drury
Lane, might well have stood in the wings and heard the dialogue in
Pizarro with gratification; observing, with a ghost's omniscience,
how they drew on the Westminster speeches which had brought his
son fame – and in which he, the teacher of elocution, could surely
claim a share. *Pizarro* also gave Sheridan a chance to weave in
music with the spectacle. Operatic or near-operatic effects were
dear to his heart: it was as much to its music as its plot and
dialogue that *The Duenna* had owed its success. *Pizarro* had a plot
and characters which demanded more serious attention, but how
important its musical effects were it is easy to tell from the elaborate stage directions alone (for those wishing to know more about
it, there is, happily, a contemporary record of the various solos,
semi-chorusus and so on).[4] Climactic moments regularly find expression in musical set-pieces: the 'solemn march' in the Temple of
the Sun (II.ii); the full-scale choruses of Priest and Virgins, the
scene (III.i) when the wives and children of the Peruvian warriors
sing alternately 'stanzas expressive of their situation, with a CHORUS,
in which all join'. The play ends on a characteristically operatic
note. A Dead March accompanies the solemn procession which
brings in Rolla's body on its bier. In a final, heroic tableau, Alonzo
and Cora kneel on either side of the bier, kissing the dead hero's
hands while the King and the rest of the company look on in
expressive silence. The Priests and Priestesses chant a funeral

dirge and to the sound of their music the curtain 'slowly descends'. It is almost *Aida*. Sheridan looks toward grand opera here, as in *The Duenna* he seemed every now and then to be anticipating the Mozart of *Don Giovanni*.

The illustration of the screen scene in *The School for Scandal* already mentioned (see Frontispiece) shows the two stage boxes occupied by a fashionable audience who are replicas – in their high head-dresses and full-skirted coats – of the actors standing remarkably close to them. The spectators in the boxes could be imagined stepping over the low parapet forming their box and fitting easily into place, along with the actors on the forestage, as spectators within the play. To a modern mind such interesting closeness sets up thoughts of meta-theatrical explorations into the elusive zone between illusion and reality. Tom Stoppard's light-hearted treatment of that motif in *The Real Inspector Hound* – where two critics observing the 'real' play are drawn into it as characters – made *Hound* a fascinatingly apt choice of partner for *The Critic* when the two plays were presented as a double bill at the National Theatre in 1985. Ayckbourn, a master of actor/audience relationships, directed Stoppard's play and Stoppard, the great illusionist, Sheridan's. It was a double that brilliantly underlined the potentiality for meta-theatrical effects in Sheridan's comedy.

In their own way both Sheridan and Goldsmith exploited this potentiality: the idea of playing a part is at the heart of their comedy, thematically as well as structurally. Kate Hardcastle sets out to play the barmaid with a deliberate reference to the theatre; Julia awaiting the dreaded visit of Captain Absolute reflects 'What a difficult scene I am now to go through'. Joseph Surface similarly contemplates the tricky hand he has to play before arranging his face suitably, to receive Lady Teazle. Both playwrights possessed a sense of the stage as a place where actors and audience came very close together, and where the actor would transform himself, harlequin fashion, under the very noses of his observers. This highly developed stage sense was a crucial factor in their comedy of subtle disguisings and improvisings.

4
Questions of Taste: Sentimental Comedy. 'The Good Natur'd Man' and 'A Trip to Scarborough'

Goldsmith's campaign against sentimental comedy was not an expression of hostility to sentiment *in* comedy. He was a man of sentiment himself, as we need look no further than his sympathetic portrayal of sentimental Mr Hardcastle to perceive. The attack was aimed quite specifically at a certain type of comedy which achieved its height of popularity in his day and can fairly be represented by such a play as Hugh Kelly's *False Delicacy* (1768). Sheridan followed Goldsmith in denigrating the 'goddess of the woeful countenance' – though with rather less fire and fury, the fate of his own plays being less affected by the sentimental vogue.

How does sentimental comedy look to a modern eye? In the first place, it was no single, homogeneous form but immensely varied. When it began to creep in, at the end of the seventeenth century, it was obviously in part a reaction against the free-spoken, bawdy sex comedy of the Restoration (which had come under fire from Jeremy Collier and the puritanical lobby). Comedy turned morally circumspect and 'nice' in the plays of Steele, who paid tribute to domestic virtue and married faithfulness in plays like *The Tender Husband* (1705). He said of his anti-duelling play, *The Lying Lover*, that in portraying the distresses of his hero in prison, he had deliberately sacrificed comedy and chosen 'with pity to chastise delight', for 'laughter's a distorted passion'. A strange remark from a writer of comedy, it must have seemed in 1703. By 1768, however, when the 'comedy of tears' was well established, it would have struck a more familiar note.

An interesting little tale of changing taste is contained in the variations played on Cibber's play, *Love's Last Shift*, between 1696, when that play appeared, and 1777 when Sheridan rewrote Vanbrugh's rewrite, *The Relapse*. Cibber's 'genteel' comedy was well tailored to the taste of his time: audiences approved his balance of foppish, sexually titillating elements with edifying exhortations to virtue. The philandering hero of *Love's Last Shift* is converted by love with unlikely suddenness. Marriage bells ring optimistically for a future of wedded bliss, which seems hardly guaranteed by his past promiscuity. That instant conversion inspired Vanbrugh to produce at top speed a sceptical 'sequel'. Its sardonic title, *The Relapse*, indicated what he thought more likely to happen to Cibber's wedded pair when honeymoon delights and romantic country retreats began to pall. Vanbrugh's Loveless soon becomes restless; the sight of a pretty woman in a theatre box sets his fancy racing and when by chance the unknown beauty visits his wife, the next step – which is his relapse – comes with little scruple on his part. Nor on hers, for although Berinthia is Amanda's friend, she feels entitled to a share in her husband, having learnt to her chagrin that her own former lover, Worthy, has turned his attention (unavailingly) to Amanda. This is the way of the world, Vanbrugh seems to say, the real, nasty world, which the optimistic moralists tried not to see. Yet such was the force of the *zeitgeist* that Vanbrugh too, for all his scepticism and tart wit, was obliged to succumb to sentiment. Though he had refused to believe in the conversion postulated by Cibber, he introduced one of his own, equally if not more improbable. In the very act of forcing himself on the virtuous Amanda, Worthy is struck to the heart by her noble resistance. The 'magic force of love', he says, has made the 'raging lion' tame and though he wonders later how long the influence will last, he assures himself that for the present at least: 'The coarser appetite of nature's gone, and 'tis, methinks, the food of angels I require.'

The final 'purification' of the fable came in 1777 when Sheridan adapted Vanbrugh's play to the decorous taste of his own time, cutting out Vanbrugh's frank portrayal of the liaison between Loveless and Berinthia and making the lady much more reticent about her free and easy sexual morality. These were acts of censorship that would have surprised Cibber no less than Vanbrugh. Yet, although perfectly aware that he might be weakening the

comedy by his concessions to a prudish audience, he probably did
not go altogether against the grain of his own personality in making these revisions.

Goldsmith seems to have felt more seriously thwarted than
Sheridan by the conventions of the time. This was hardly surprising: one of his supreme virtues as a writer, his naturalness, was
threatened by the gentility and refinement required even of comic
writers. 'Let us, instead of trying to write finely, write naturally',
he pleaded at the close of a chapter on literary decay in his essay of
1759, *Enquiry into the Present State of Polite Learning in Europe*.
This was written before he made his first venture into the theatre,
but in discussing the difficulty of handling certain 'natural' subjects, he put his finger on just the spot that was to cause him
trouble with *The Good Natur'd Man*:

> Does the poet paint the absurdities of the vulgar; then he is
> *low*; does he exaggerate the features of folly, to render it
> more thoroughly ridiculous, he is then *very* low.

The poet was only allowed to exercise his comic or satirical gifts,
complained Goldsmith, on subjects from 'high life' and this was
hard because:

> Among well-bred fools we may despise much but have little
> to laugh at; nature seems to present us with an universal
> blank of silk, ribbands, smiles and whispers: absurdity is the
> poet's game, and good breeding is the nice concealment of
> absurdities.[1]

We may detect in this a suggestion of the Irishman's bafflement
and irritation at the phlegm of the complacent 'well-bred' English
middle class, their insistence on keeping up polite appearances at
all costs. The gentility of audiences threatened to bar him from
expressing a large part of his roving, impecunious, boldly varied
life experience. In his preface to *The Good Natur'd Man* Goldsmith imagined himself speaking to readers more robust than
audiences had proved. The term, '*genteel comedy*', was unknown
when he wrote the play, he said; public taste had changed and
'grown of late, perhaps, too delicate'. He could only hope that 'too
much refinement will not banish humour and character from our's

as it has already done from the French theatre' (in the process, so he claimed, banishing spectators too – perhaps a piece of wishful thinking).

Just before his second play was performed, Goldsmith returned to the attack, portraying the 'genteel' drama as a perversion of comedy in 'An Essay on the Theatre: or A Comparison between Laughing and Sentimental Comedy' (*Westminster Magazine*, December 1772, vol. 1).[2] Why had comedy more or less banished the 'pompous train' and 'swelling phrase' of tragedy from the contemporary stage, he asked. Surely because comedy was more open to all kinds of people. It was the 'natural portrait of human folly and frailty, of which all are judges, because all have sat for the picture'. 'Natural', that Rousseauesque word is, as so often with Goldsmith, the key word of praise. But there was a problem in copying from nature. She presents a 'double face, either of mirth or sadness' and contemporary writers, so he suggested, were 'at a loss which chiefly to copy from'. Goldsmith was prepared to acknowledge that there was a serious debate taking place on the question 'whether the exhibition of human distress is likely to afford the mind more entertainment than that of human absurdity'. The comment is not merely ironic. He knew (if only from Shakespeare) that comedy with sad or thoughtful aspects could entertain. And he admitted that 'these sentimental pieces do often amuse us'. But his need to protect his own comic freedoms prevents him from doing more than glance at the radical shift of form implicit in the sentimental comedies of his time.

That he recognised something of the radicalism (if only to find it damaging) is suggested by his summing up of the new genre: 'a new species of dramatic composition has been introduced, under the name of *sentimental* comedy, in which the virtues of private life are exhibited, rather than the vices exposed; and the distresses rather than the faults of mankind make our interest in the piece.'

A closer look at the distinguishing features of sentimental comedy may show how far from simple was Goldsmith's relationship with the new genre. He had something in common with writers like Cumberland and Kelly as well as points of difference; inevitably, since sentimental comedy represented a deep change taking place in the national psyche. It was a response to eighteenth-century society's wish to reform and refine itself, along lines which should appeal to us today. Plays such as *The Clandestine Marriage*,

The West Indian and *False Delicacy* called on society to be fairer
and kinder, especially in its treatment of women. The movement
may have had its censorious, puritanical side but it also served a
benevolent purpose by providing models of humane behaviour.
Feminine sensibility was given more scope. Where Restoration
playwrights had used satire to cast a mocking light on social
absurdities and hypocrisies, usually from the perspective of witty
young male characters, the sentimentalists liked to focus, as Goldsmith said, on the distresses caused by society's unfairness. Marriage, that perennial problem, was put under a new spotlight, with
a stronger emphasis on women's suffering as victims of a hard-
nosed, often hypocritical bourgeois society. Elopements and secret love matches loom large in plots and women characters'
attempts at rebellion are treated more softly and sympathetically
than in the basically sardonic comedy of the Restoration. Romantic love comes to the fore, as in *The Clandestine Marriage*, where
the emotional heroine's sensibility sets the tone for the play's
moral conclusion.

The theatre in effect took over a whole new outlook on social
arrangements and sexual preconceptions, responding to ideas fer-
menting in this, the age of Rousseau, the Contrat Social and the
run-up to the French Revolution. No individual play of Kelly or
Cumberland or Garrick/Colman could be described as exactly
revolutionary but there was nevertheless a quiet revolution taking
place in the thrust of the genre they were creating. The middle-
class people who sat in the boxes and pit at Covent Garden were
demanding to be taken seriously; in earlier comedy they had more
often been targets for satire and ridicule. Goldsmith subscribed to
the orthodox literary view of his day that suffering was for tragedy
and tragedy must be concerned only with the 'great': 'We do not so
strongly sympathise with one born in humbler circumstances.' He
wanted to penetrate into 'the recesses of the mean' but thought
comedy the only appropriate way of doing so. Theatre audiences
thought differently. They were already reading novels which had
burst through conventional class limits. Richardson's *Pamela*, an
enormously influential novel, had focused on the emotional distresses of a servant girl sexually harassed by an upper-class cad
whom she eventually reforms and marries. Theatre audiences
were not quite ready for plays centred on the working classes: that
was reserved for the nineteenth-century melodrama to accom-

plish. But they were prepared for their comedy to take in serious crises of feeling. If a new form had to be invented – a hybrid of the comic and the tragic – so be it; they were ready to cry as well as laugh in the course of the one play, even if it were described (misleadingly, according to Goldsmith) as a comedy. Melodrama – another serious but non-tragic form – was clearly on the horizon in these last decades of the century, while beyond it the outline of the Ibsenite realistic drama can be faintly discerned.

The French term *drame* sometimes looks the most appropriate one for the new hybrid. French influence was certainly strong on the English sentimental comedy. The French *comedie larmoyante* (itself inspired partly by Richardson's 'feminine' novels) invited the audience to open their hearts to the softer emotions, be prepared to cry with pity, laugh without derision. Goldsmith, as we have seen, was especially scornful of this comedy of tears. There was one French playwright, however, whom he did not dismiss – scarcely could have done, since the comedies of Marivaux had much in common with his own. One of the most celebrated, *Le Jeu de l'amour et du hasard* (1730), is clearly in the background of *She Stoops to Conquer* (if filtered through other sources). Marivaux provided a piquant model for a comedy of mistakes and disguisings. He wrote for the Italian Players in Paris; not a fortuitous connection, for the game-playing in which his characters exuberantly indulge derives directly from the *commedia dell'arte*. The subversive Italian 'masks' make their way into his urbane eighteenth-century settings, often under their traditional names: Harlequin, pre-eminently. Almost everyone on his stage seems to be acting or playing with the idea of acting. 'False Impressions', the English version of one of his titles, exactly places a ruling preoccupation of his comedy: the difficulty people have in understanding each other – and themselves – especially in matters of love and sex.

Acting in the world of Marivaux, though partly frivolous and comic, is essentially a step to understanding. So, in *Le Jeu de l'amour et du hasard* Silvia, awaiting the arrival of the young man designated as her husband (she has never met him), asks a favour of her kind but authoritarian father: 'What if I could see him, examine him a little without his knowing who I am?' She proposes to pass herself off as her own servant, Lisette, an idea which amuses her father. He tells himself: 'If I let her do it, something quite unique is bound to happen. Something she isn't expecting herself.' What happens is odd if not unique. The intended husband, Dorante, equally eager not to buy a pig in a poke, persuades his servant, Harlequin, to change places with him. So the affianced upper-class pair meet each other as servants, the servants meet as master and mistress, and in this disconcerting way they surprise each other into genuine understanding of their real natures. By acting roles unfamiliar to them, the comedy suggests, they reveal themselves all the more clearly. The false social impressions cannot conceal the vulgarity of the servants, the gentility of the upper-class lovers. Despite the jarring effect of its attitude to class differences, the comedy strikes a modern note in its ingenious use of play-acting to probe into the self behind the facade. This was material with rich potentiality for the English sentimental playwrights, all so interested in drawing lines between genuine and affected behaviour. Goldsmith was in tune with them in this respect. His original title for *She Stoops to Conquer*, 'The Mistakes of a Night' is in Marivaux vein as, more importantly, is one of his key situations, Kate Hardcastle's testing of Marlow. Like an English Silvia, she acts a servant's part in her own home, giving herself a freedom otherwise denied her, to learn more about the character of the man her father means her to marry.

The sophistication of the sexual games in Marivaux' comedy (deftly brought out in modern English productions by directors like Bill Gaskill and Mike Alfreds) was probably beyond the scope of the eighteenth-century English writers of sentimental comedy. They took up with relish, however, the idea that a comedy plot based on 'False Impressions' (with all its opportunities for farce) could be used to explore seriously into states of feeling. They tended only to touch the surface of inner emotional experience (Hugh Kelly goes further than most in *False Delicacy*) but they made much of the danger to society in the mistaken ideas people could hold about each other. Richard Cumberland's *The West Indian* (1771), for example, is a comedy of mistakes which keeps general social issues to the fore. The plot turns on the particularly embarrassing mistake made by a young man from the West Indies, new to London, who is misled into taking an innocent girl of good family for a kept woman. He proposes a liaison to her, explaining kindly that he likes her enough to marry her if her social situation were other than it is. When he discovers his gaffe and pleads forgiveness, Belcour is given a mighty lecture by Louisa (who is in love with him, despite all):

> Upon the part of virtue I'm not empowered to speak, but if hereafter, as you range through life, you should surprise her in the person of some wretched female, poor as myself and not so well protected, enforce not your advantage, complete not your licentious triumph, but raise her, rescue her from shame and sorrow, and reconcile her to herself again.

Melodrama is not far off here. Another comedy of Cumberland's, *The Fashionable Lover* (1772), takes a step nearer still. The heroine, Augusta Aubrey, has her life nearly ruined by a mistake that threatens her virtuous reputation. Like the heroines of Dion Boucicault, master of the melodrama to come, she is a victim of economic as well as sexual attack. The vulgar Bridgemore has cheated her out of her inheritance, and Lord Abberville compromises her unfeelingly. He makes his way uninvited into her sitting room in the Bridgemore house, where she is living on sufferance, locks the door and forces her to listen to his declaration of love. When the jealous Lucinda Bridgemore demands entrance, made suspicious by the locked door, the situation takes a turn familiar in Restoration comedy, with the would-be seducer hiding in the bedroom. But the emotional impression here is in another world – much closer to that of the morally-oriented melodrama. 'Where shall I turn myself?', Augusta says to her arrogant admirer, as he prepares to hide: 'You've ruined all: if you're discovered, I shall never gain belief.' The difficulty of gaining 'belief', of correcting the 'false impression' dominates the plot, as so often in sentimental comedy. How are even Augusta's sympathisers to know that the Bridgemores' accusation is unjustified? Similarly in *The West Indian*, how can the crossed lines be uncrossed, what does it take before people can be seen for what they really are?

Cumberland liked to appeal to his audience for fair play for minority groups (women counting as such, though no doubt larger in numbers than men, then as now). England's honour looms large in these appeals. The brash hero of *The West Indian* deserves a sympathetic hearing, the prologue suggests, for 'sure that country has no feeble claim/Which swells your commerce, and supports your fame'. Politics could not intrude into English drama in any controversial way (the Licensing Act of 1737 had seen to that) but Cumberland touches occasionally on the political implications of social issues, even to the point of urging mild reform. In *The Note of Hand*, mentioned earlier as a near melodrama in its scenic strategies, the gambling addiction of Young Rivers is pointedly related to the misery endured by his tenants. He is the absentee landlord of an estate in Ireland which his neglect is helping to destroy. One of the tenants, MacCormuck, has journeyed to England to remonstrate with Rivers – whom he last saw as a boy. Not recognising him when they meet in the Newmarket inn where the action is set, he explains his mission to the apparent stranger in terms which bring home to the already chastened Rivers the enormity of his offence: 'We, that are his poor tenants in Ireland, have taken full as much offence at him, as he can with us; – rack, rack, – drain, drain – and here's the gulph that swallows it; (*looking into the gaming room*).

Cumberland makes a political point when Rivers asks MacCormuck a naïve question; what does he think of England, the 'sister kingdom'? The answer may have caused some ripples in the audience:

> Why, I think you've got all the inheritance to yourselves, and that it would be but charity to throw us a rag of clothes to kiver our nakedness; by my soul, Mr Rivers, it would be for the honour of the family and a christian-like action into the bargain.

The appeal to 'family' feeling is characteristic. Cumberland, along with other sentimentalists, has a primarily optimistic view of the state of the nation. There is a fascination with the idea of the 'United Kingdom'. The different racial groups within the British jurisdiction – Scots, Welsh, Irish – play a prominent part in the comedies. They may be there to add to the fun with their eccentric dialects but the caricature is clearly intended as friendly, a 'family joke'. It is all part of the energetic scrutiny of itself as a community in which the theatre of the 1770s delighted. Audiences were encouraged to be open to the new, to see their age as one of social and economic change. Garrick, ever with his ear to the ground, expressed that feeling in his prologue to Sheridan's adaptation of *The Relapse* (an adaptation necessary precisely because sensibility had changed so markedly in the half century since Vanbrugh):

Men, women, children, houses, signs and fashions,
State, stage, trade, taste, the humours and the passions,
Th'Exchange, Change alley, whereso'er you're ranging,
Court, city, country, all are chang'd, or changing;

The term 'sentimental' in the context I have sketched looks rather
different from the term as Goldsmith used it. Originally it had no
pejorative sense but simply referred to 'sentiments', that is, ideas
and expressions of feeling. We should perhaps think of Kelly's
plays as leaning toward the French *drame*, Cumberland's toward
nineteenth-century melodrama. Goldsmith saw it differently, primarily because he feared the baleful effect of this social seriousness on the robust comedy and farce for which he was so gifted.
Alarm at this possibility is in the background of all his strictures.
Sentimental comedy, he maintained, denied a place to farce or
hearty humour. It was a bastard; a mis-mating between comedy
and tragedy, a 'kind of *mulish* production, with all the defects of its
opposite parents, and marked with sterility'. There was an unre-
solvable conflict between 'weeping sentimental comedy' and the
'laughing, and even low comedy, which seems to have been last
exhibited by Vanbrugh and Cibber'.[3]

Goldsmith did not scruple to ascribe the worst motives to both
writers and audiences who cultivated the new form. It was popular
with writers, he surmised, because so easy to write: anyone who
could 'hammer out a novel' could produce the necessary 'insipid
dialogue, without character or humour'. By giving his characters
'mighty good hearts' along with fine clothes, a 'pathetic scene or
two' and a 'sprinkling of tender melancholy conversation', the
sentimentalist could make the ladies cry and the gentlemen applaud. The spectators liked it because it flattered them: 'In these
plays almost all the characters are good, and exceedingly generous; they are lavish enough of their *tin* money on the stage' (a
cry from the heart here, given Goldsmith's bitter experiences in
money matters). At the same time, he says, the morality in the
plays is suspect. Folly is not ridiculed and audiences are asked not
only to pardon but to applaud any faults characters may have 'in
consideration of the goodness of their hearts'. This makes the new
comedy seem a very soppy affair: Goldsmith's satiric pen did not
fail, driven as it was by the need to protect the 'true' comedy. Is
there not room for both, he reflects at one point in his essay; what
if sentimental comedy went under some other name, why deny the

audience 'that or any other innocent pleasure'? But he dismisses
the 'objections' as specious, returning, as ever, to the crux: sentimental comedy is driving true comedy from the stage:

> it will soon happen that our comic players will have nothing
> left for it but a fine coat and a song. It depends upon the
> audience whether they will actually drive those poor merry
> creatures from the stage, or sit at a play as gloomy as at the
> Tabernacle.[4]

Was humour really so lacking in sentimental comedy? In fact
Garrick and Colman had shown that the two could go together in
their very successful *The Clandestine Marriage*. This comedy
appeared in 1766, only two years before Goldsmith's *The Good
Natur'd Man* and at once established itself as one of the most
popular plays of the period. It has retained its power to amuse, as
anyone who saw Alastair Sim as a deliciously pawky Lord Ogleby
will surely agree. *The Clandestine Marriage* is one of the few plays
from the last decades of the eighteenth century, other than Goldsmith's or Sheridan's, to be revived on the modern English stage;
sufficient proof that it has comic appeal.

It is also, however, a thoroughly sentimental play, in the sense
that Goldsmith had in mind when he spoke of 'mighty good
hearts', 'a pathetic scene or two' and 'a sprinkling of tender,
melancholy conversation'. Lord Ogleby, the aged roué, who
patches and paints and calls on his French valet for flattering
assurances that he is still attractive to young women, is from one
angle a familiar comic character, almost straight out of a Restoration satire. But – here the ways divide – we can only laugh at him
up to a point. He turns out to have the heart of gold which
Goldsmith despised as an ubiquitous item in sentimental comedy.
By the end of the play he and Fanny, the quintessential sentimental heroine, have formed a benevolent conspiracy which
frees the girl from the base greed and envy motivating the rest of
her family. Comical elements in *The Clandestine Marriage* are
skilfully kept within the bounds of gentility. Gentility is indeed
the theme, in the variation favoured by the sentimentalists;
true 'gentleness' contrasted with pretensions to the 'genteel'.
Mr Sterling, the wealthy businessman whose plans to marry his

daughters power the plot, thinks he can buy gentility as he buys landscaping for his garden. His brash assurance that money is everything makes for some very funny scenes, as when, in Act II.i, he insists on taking poor rheumaticky old Lord Ogleby round his latest 'improvements' before breakfast, pushing aside Mrs Heidel-berg's demurral, 'You'll absolutely fatigue his lordship with over-walking, brother':

Sterling:	I'll only show his lordship my ruins, and the cascade, and the Chinese bridge, and then we'll go in to breakfast.
Lord Ogleby:	Ruins, did you say, Mr Sterling?
Sterling:	Ay, ruins, my Lord! and they are reckoned very fine ones too. You would think them ready to tumble on your head. It has just cost me a hundred and fifty pounds to put my ruins in thorough repair, – This way, if your lordship pleases.

Comedy survives, despite Goldsmith's fears, but it is firmly bound up with sentiment. Sterling's mercenariness is shown to cause distress, above all to his younger daughter, Fanny, a girl of 'amiable delicacy' and fine feeling. She has already secretly thwarted her father's intentions to buy both his daughters rich upper-class husbands with his 'stuff' (as he calls his money) by marrying penniless Lovewell, whom she loves romantically. In one of the play's most biting scenes, Sterling accepts a financial bribe from the intended husband of his elder daughter, to break the agreed marriage contract and put Fanny (with whom Sir John has fallen in love) in her sister's place. Sir John is very business-like in his approach to the awkward matter of throwing over his affianced bride. He surmises – rightly – that the offer to her father of an extra thirty thousand pounds will do the trick. But he is no longer the man who entered the contract with an eye only to business, who was ready to 'receive one woman as soon as another'. His passion for Fanny has made him a convert to love, though, as he tells Lovewell, he formerly 'looked upon love, serious, sober love, as a chimaera, and marriage as a thing of course, as you know most people do'.

That phrase 'as you know most people do' invites the audience to examine their own attitudes to this burning issue. They are guided to the right point of view through their expected sympathy for Fanny, the 'sport' of the Sterling family, who suffers agonies at 'the indelicacy of a secret marriage' (Lovewell's wish to secure their financial future is responsible). Fanny is no feminist. To modern taste she seems indeed excessively prone to shame and embarrassment over her plight. Still, the plight is real enough: she is pregnant and feels obliged to keep the secret as long as she can, even from Lovewell, so as not to impede his strategies for improving their position.

The male authors evidently had some reservations about Fanny's feminine sensibility. She is made at one point to ask Lovewell's forgiveness for 'this weakness, this delicacy – this what you will'. But in the main her sensitivity is her recommendation to the sympathies of the audience. It is she, the rebel against the business approach to marriage, who sets the moral tone. When she lectures Sir John on his 'blackest treachery' to her sister, she does not alienate but enchants him. Her 'scruples and delicacy' are part of her charm for him, as they are for Lord Ogleby who becomes infatuated with her too. Broad comedy enters robustly in the scene where she approaches him for help against a forced marriage and he thinks he has made a conquest (IV.i). He is so vain – and she so delicately obscure in her confession – that he is able to misinterpret her appeal as a declaration of love. When he learns that the 'rash action which passion prompted, and modesty has long concealed' was in fact the clandestine marriage with Lovewell, he proves himself to be, despite his absurdities, a man of feeling. It is a blow, but he reacts as a true gentleman should (such is the suggestion), honourably and with compassion: 'Poor girl! I swore to support her affection with my life and fortune – 'tis a debt of honour, and must be paid.' He is not a Restoration roué, after all – though the clever authors contrived to draw that sort of comedy from him.

The Clandestine Marriage might seem to disprove Goldsmith's assertion that sentimental comedy was inimical to humour. We should note, however, that its fun is kept well within the bounds demanded by audiences of the time. It does not involve a penetration of the 'mean' into the sphere of the refined. Refined elements came increasingly to the fore in the years that followed and by 1768, when Goldsmith made his entry into the theatre, sentimental comedy had reached new levels of concentration on the strange workings of sensibility. Goldsmith must have thought his suspicions of the genre justified when Garrick rejected his own first offering in favour of Hugh Kelly's *False Delicacy*, a play that epitomised the sentimental genre in its latest phase. Whereas in *The Clandestine Marriage*, Fanny stands out as uniquely sensitive, in *False Delicacy* every character has the capacity for refined feeling; some take it too far, some modify it with common sense, none is totally insensitive. Simple comical contrasts based on the crudity of a character like Sterling give way to an interest in degrees of refinement. Kelly likes to explore in the grey areas where benign sensitivity shades into a more extreme, even neurotic kind. There is food for amusement here, but it is more ambivalent and dry.

Garrick compounded his unfriendly act (as no doubt Goldsmith thought it) by contriving to put *False Delicacy* on stage at Drury Lane just ahead of *The Good Natur'd Man* at Covent Garden. Kelly's play had by far the greater success: it was a hit in France, where it appealed to a public taste formed by Marivaux and the *comédie larmoyante*. Does this mean that it has to be seen as the quintessential sentimental comedy so detested by Goldsmith – with a dearth of humour and a plethora of boringly good-hearted people? Was it (as should follow) as unlike as possible to *The Good Natur'd Man*? Criticism has tended to assume so: the play has been dismissed with epithets like 'washy' or 'mawkish' and seen as simply proving Goldsmith's point about the unfunniness and flatness of sentimental comedy.

Yet it is far from being so simple. *False Delicacy*, as its title suggests, is concerned to a great extent with extremes and the view is at least partly ironic. As in *The Clandestine Marriage*, the misunderstandings and crossed lines which make the plot result from a scrupulous sense of what is proper. The resulting absurdities are not overlooked by Kelly (after all, he was Irish too, as we are reminded in the epilogue which jokes about his 'false modesty'). His comedy is muted, however, usually taking the form of amused comments by the more down-to-earth characters on the soul-searching of the rest. It would have to be admitted that the dialogue has its longueurs. These genteel beings are maddeningly well-behaved for rather too long at a stretch; their language is pompous and their absorption in their own consciences can become tedious. Goldsmith's gibes had some basis in fact. Yet the twists and turns of their self-questioning and self-scourging acquire a curious validity, even a quiet charm, which makes the occasional outbursts of more 'normal' impulsive behaviour (for example, ardent Sir Harry's refusal to accept his girl's change of mind about eloping) seem coarse and egotistical.

False Delicacy turns, in the usual way, on a catastrophic mistake. Lady Betty Lambton, just before the play begins, has refused an offer of marriage from the man she loves. Why does she do anything so strange? The play opens, characteristically, with a discussion of the puzzle. The dialogue begins in the middle of the conversation with Sidney, friend of the rejected Lord Winworth, surmising: 'Still, I can't help thinking but Lady Betty Lambton's refusal was infinitely more the result of an extraordinary delicacy, than the want of an affection for your lordship.' He is right, though Lord Winworth is too modest to accept the need for such an explanation. Lady Betty knows too well that she has been, as she says, 'a fool'. Yet she had her reasons; she is a widow, and as she confides to her confidante, Mrs Harley, the unhappiness of her first marriage made her 'resolve against another'. So far, so understandable; but she becomes harder to follow when she reveals her underlying thought that 'a woman of real delicacy should never admit a second impression on her heart'. Mrs Harley has no doubt that this is hyper-sensitive: 'Well, the devil take this delicacy; I don't know anything it does besides making people miserable.' The reaction was obviously intended to draw laughter from an audience more likely to be in tune with Mrs Harley's practical outlook than Lady Betty's romantic scruples.

Yet Kelly meant his audience to see the attractive as well as the absurd side of this delicate feeling. Mrs Harley makes this clear when she follows up her tart comment – 'Well, thank heaven my sentiments are not sufficiently refin'd to make me unhappy' – with the concession, 'And yet somehow, foolish as it is, one can't help liking it.' What is there to like in it? A very positive side of Lady Betty's refinement is her consideration for the orphaned Miss Marchmont. She not only gives her a home but is keenly sensitive to what she imagines her feelings to be, tries to avoid hurting her pride and would never injure her prospects. Her fine feeling becomes a source of pain when Lord Winworth approaches her again. Despairing of Lady Betty, he has proposed to Miss Marchmont (as the next best thing) and seeks Lady Betty's help in persuading the girl (who is secretly in love with Sidney) to accept him. There follows a bitter-sweet contest in moral delicacy, as each woman struggles to put the other's supposed interests before her own. Miss Marchmont had at first refused Lord Winworth, to Lady Betty's well-concealed delight. Then – consternation – she takes back her refusal, accusing herself of ingratitude to her patron who seems so anxious for the match (Lady Betty has performed too well). Kelly manages to inject some convincingly less-than-noble reactions into all this magnanimity. Lady Betty admits to Mrs Harley that her over-ardent support of Lord Winworth to Miss Marchmont owed something to pique: 'greatly as I dreaded her approbation of the proposal, – I was secretly hurt at her insensibility to the personal attractions of his lordship.' 'I don't doubt it, my dear' is Mrs Harley's equally believable reply. 'We think all the world should love what we are in love with ourselves.'

False Delicacy offers many 'sentimental' perspectives on stock situations. There is the man of fifty in love with the girl of twenty, the situation found so ludicrous (and irresistible, by Restoration playwrights). Kelly makes his Cecil an attractive figure, jovially irascible about new-fangled ways and fashions like giving children pompous names ('By and by we shan't have a Ralph or a Roger, a Bridget or an Alice, remaining in the kingdom'). The scene in which he proposes, as if on behalf of another, to Miss Marchmont – 'Why, what do you think of a man about my age?' – is clearly meant to have the audience's sympathy (Tom King, the actor, had already asked for it in the prologue, we may recall). She responds with gentleness and gives such a touching account of her inability to upset her 'benefactress' by confessing her love for Sidney that she has Cecil feeling for his handkerchief: 'You are a good girl, a very good girl.' Another familiar situation, that of the girl resisting an arranged marriage, is given a push towards good feeling. When the authoritarian Mr Rivers catches his daughter in the act of eloping (while waiting for her unpunctual lover) he casts her off from his affections but honours his promise to settle money on her, thrusting into her hand a pocket book with twenty thousand pounds in it. This so touches her conscience that she instantly abandons the elopement – and is only saved by the intervention of Cecil from being abducted by her indignant lover; the nearest to a violent action the comedy allows.

All the complications are resolved with the aid of sensible Cecil and Mrs Harley. Lady Betty retrieves her mistake, the four pairs of lovers are sorted out as they would wish, and the play ends on the optimistic note characteristic of sentimental comedy, with Mr Rivers announcing that 'those who generously labour for the happiness of others will, sooner or later, arrive at happiness themselves'. We have seen that Garrick's prologue spread a safety net by having Tom King deliver a mock diatribe against scribblers who *would* write 'moral plays'. A popular comedian, 'Tom Fool', was required by the 'strange, awkward bard' to go outside his usual line of business and shed tears. Would he be able to do it? He invited his fans to be interested in the idea:

> Do, ladies, look upon me – nay, no simp'ring –
> Think you this face was ever made for whimp'ring?

The lines were to be echoed by Sheridan in his satirical prologue to *The Rivals* and the sentiments were quite in tune with Goldsmith's, which shows how much hesitation and ambivalence there was on all sides. Characters were often made to poke fun at the sentimental genre from within the plays: Cumberland's Revell scolds his friend for being dull, 'dull as a sentimental comedy'. And the theatre managers liked to hedge their bets, as Garrick did with his prologue to Kelly's play. He was equivocal about its plethora of sentiment, while Colman was nervous about Goldsmith's lack of it.

In fact there is no such huge gap between *The Good-Natur'd Man* and *False Delicacy* as Goldsmith's attacks on the sentimental genre might have led his audience to expect. Or rather, there is a gulf, but it is to do with language and style rather than the presence or absence of edifying sentiment. Goldsmith's play is every bit as 'moral' as Kelly's. It is that favourite with English audiences, an 'education' play. Young Honeywood is one of the erring young men dear to the eighteenth-century heart, who spend most of the stage time behaving foolishly or recklessly, usually wasting money, and are finally brought to realise their mistakes, with the aid of guardians or older relatives who have been keeping a watchful eye on them all the time; Cumberland's Young Rivers in *The Note of Hand* is one and Belcour in *The West Indian* another (his 'monitor', Stockwell, reveals himself as his father once the youth has reformed). The reformation in Goldsmith's play is as total as in any of them. Honeywood accepts his uncle's final rebukes with abject self-condemnation: 'Yes, sir, I now too plainly perceive my errors. My vanity, in attempting to please all by fearing to offend any. My meanness, in approving folly lest fools should disapprove.'

Goldsmith too had his crossed lines, false impressions – and an attempted elopement. Like the lovers in *False Delicacy*, his Leontine and Olivia are surprised in the act of eloping by a stern but basically well-meaning father who eventually allows himself to be talked round. Goldsmith had a genuine interest in elopements (he was later to write an essay on 'Scotch Marriages' in the persona of a landlady deploring the practice). But his handling of the elopement material in his play owes more to theatre convention than life. The 'false impression' created as a blind by Leontine and Olivia is one of the most improbable on a stage which had seen a good many such. We can believe that Leontine has fallen in love with a girl he met in France and brought her home instead of the sister he was sent out for; but hardly that he would succeed in passing the stranger off as his sister, even to their own parents. The implausible deceit, kept going by artificial coincidences, stagey letters and the like, made it hard for the actors to hit the natural note which is achieved elsewhere in the play. A contemporary reviewer's comment that Goldsmith's 'fable' was unsatisfactory seems right in relation to the Leontine/Olivia episode.

The rub of the play is not in that love plot, however, large though the elopement looms in the stage action, but in the strange story of the good-natured man, Young Honeywood. Rousseauesque ideas of nature are curiously tested here; and Goldsmith draws on his own life with a candour that would be obvious to all in the audience who knew him. It would have been most obvious in Act III.i, where the bailiffs turn up to arrest Honeywood for debt and Goldsmith enjoys himself by making them comic but also rather fearsomely believable characters. The chief bailiff's highly developed sense of social superiority comes from having so much to do with the gentry:

Bailiff: Looky, sir, I have arrested as good men as you in my time: no disparagement of you neither. Men that would go forty guineas on a game of

cribbage. I challenge the town to show a man in
more genteeler practice than myself!

Honeywood: Without all question, Mr. – I forget your name,
sir?

Bailiff: How can you forget what you never knew? he,
he, he!

The first night audience presumably writhed at these jovial fam-
iliarities, and at the ironic emphasis the word 'gentleman' acquired
when Twitch (the name he finally admits to) accepted Honeywood's bribe to pass himself and his follower off as his friends:
'I'm sure no man can say I ever give a gentleman that was a
gentleman, ill usage. If I saw that a gentleman was a gentleman, I
have taken money not to see him for ten weeks together.' Goldsmith hits his distinctive note in the playfulness of this scene. All
are acting, from Honeywood himself (desperate to hide his humiliating situation from Miss Richland when she unexpectedly calls)
to the second bailiff, Little Flanigan, who is fitted with a costume
for his 'gentleman's' role from Honeywood's wardrobe. Flanigan,
so Twitch says, has acted as 'master of ceremonies to the black
queen of Morocco'. The reference (to puppet shows) hints at a
taste for holding the stage, which Honeywood tries in vain to
suppress. Like a nervous director, he begs Twitch to keep his
follower quiet and himself say nothing without being directed. But
Flanigan is irrepressible: 'Never you fear me, I'll show the lady
that I have something to say for myself as well as another. One
man has one way of talking, and another man has another, that's
all the difference between them.'

The scene is a good test of Miss Richland's quick-wittedness and
sense of humour. She may have seemed to the contemporary
audience even too quick, for a well-bred young lady, to guess the
real nature of the 'odd-looking' men whom Honeywood intro-
duces as 'two of my very good friends' (her maid is allowed to
place them more exactly at the end of the scene). Miss Richland is
too high-spirited and intelligent to close her eyes to the mess
Honeywood is in – or to its more absurd aspects. She is in love with
him and takes his plight seriously enough to pay his debts later on;
but she has some fun with it first. A witty sub-text of thrust and
parry develops, with Honeywood using all his ingenuity to cover
up the trade talk ('good circuit weather', 'course of law', 'habeas

corpus') by which the bailiffs give themselves away. He shows himself capable of witty flights during these improvisations. The two are officers, he says, who have been 'upon very disagreeable duty'. When Miss Richland demurely enquires, 'The gentlemen are in the marine service, I presume, sir?', he comes back with a smart pun: 'Why madam, they do – occasionally serve in the Fleet, madam! A dangerous service!' It is a set of wit well played. They lob the ball back and forth in a high-flown discussion of literature, which, far from silencing the bailiffs, provides them with wonderfully droll conversational openings. The mention of French critics is enough to set off a flood of francophobia. 'Damn the French', says Flanigan, 'the parle vous, and all that belongs to them!' Twitch agrees, giving his subordinate encouragement to blame all the country's economic ills on the 'parle vous': 'What makes the bread rising: the parle vous that devour us. What makes the mutton fivepence a pound; the parle vous that eat it up. What makes the beer three pence halfpenny a pot –.'

Perhaps the hint of social discontent from the bailiffs had something to do with the audience's dislike of the scene (though the criticism of the French might have been expected to go down well). 'Coarse characters should be touched with a delicate pencil.' The reviewer's comment expressed a general eighteenth-century unease about scenes that went too far into 'the recesses of the mean'. Anything might happen when social boundaries were blurred as Honeywood attempts to blur them. The Covent Garden audience were certainly not prepared to believe that 'one man has one way of talking and another has another, that's all the difference between them'. Their distaste for the episode resulted in its being withdrawn from performance (though retained in the published version). They had lost not only the funniest scene in the play but one of the best demonstrations of Goldsmith's skill (generally admitted by the first reviewers of the play) in delineating character. The actors must have regretted the loss of the spirited dialogue. Powell and Mrs Bulkley also lost a chance to hint at the existence of a real, quite tender rapport between Honeywood and Miss Richland, under their playful badinage. We could imagine him giving her an appealing look when he makes one of his most absurd attempts to paraphrase the bailiffs respectably, and she laughing to herself as she tells him, surely not unkindly, that she knows just what he is up to:

Honeywood:	My dear Mr Twitch, I discern what you'd be at perfectly, and I believe the lady must be sensible of the art with which it is introduced. I suppose you perceive the meaning, madam, of his 'course of law'?
Miss Richland:	I protest, sir, I do not. I perceive only that you answer one gentleman before he has finished, and the other before he has well begun!

We can see from their lively interchanges that they may be right for each other, after all. She is someone capable of dealing with his fatal tendency to act; to act his feelings, most disastrously. It is in this area that we should look for the 'fable' which the reviewer identified as a weakness of the play. It would have to be admitted that Goldsmith obscures it by having the two love plots connect across each other in such a complicated way and by filling the stage with an assortment of comical characters who do not always fit very convincingly into either plot. Audiences enjoyed these characters, however. Goldsmith, writing with the talents of a stock company in mind, naturally provided sizeable parts for the leading comedians, Woodward and Shuter. Woodward's Lofty, forever offering to work wonders for his friends through his mythical acquaintance with powers-that-be was considered very droll – and novel, a high term of praise from audiences accustomed to much recycling of stock types. Shuter's irascible Croaker was similarly admired. Even on the page it is easy to see how the actor could have made entertainment from Croaker's exaggerated pessimism and chauvinist grumbles (which have more than a little in common with the bailiffs' francophobia). A passing comment on the weather in Act I is enough to set him off on a jeremiad: 'Indeed what signifies what weather we have in a country going to rack and ruin like ours? Taxes rising and trade falling. Money flying out of the kingdom and Jesuits swarming into it. I know at this time no less than an hundred and twenty-seven Jesuits between Charing-cross and Temple-bar.' Shuter had a part tailored for him in Croaker; no need here for little warnings about a stock actor going beyond his normal scope. The 'incendiary letter' seeking money for the planned elopement, which Croaker in Act IV misreads as a threat to blow his house up, was a particular success. Shuter was said indeed to have saved the play by his brilliantly funny playing of the incident. He can be imagined rolling his eyes in baffled rage when reading out the incomprehensible conclusion to the seeming black-mail (penned, in fact, by Garnet, the maid assisting the eloping lovers): 'But may Cupid, the little God of Love, go with you wherever you go.' 'Cupid, the little God of Love go with me!', he explodes: 'Go you to the devil, you and your little Cupid together; I'm so frightened, I scarce know whether I sit, stand or go.'

Croaker's determination to marry his son to his rich ward brings the two love plots together in a way that involves more acting – and provides the first demonstration of Honeywood's over-readiness to put 'universal benevolence' before real love. The marriage is not, says Croaker, 'much relish'd, either by one side or t'other'. Honeywood's 'fine serious advice' might persuade Leon-tine to propose and the lady to accept: she has 'a very exalted opinion of your understanding'. And though in Act I he had confessed to a 'hopeless passion' for Miss Richland, Honeywood agrees. He is not called on for that particular sacrifice, as Leontine has decided to play a part and pretend to propose, confident that Miss Richland will reject him because she is in love with Honey-wood (everyone seems to know this but Honeywood). Gold-smith showed his comic invention here in an episode Sheridan admired: he played a variation on it in *The Rivals*. Croaker stands at his son's elbow, urging him first to show more passion ('Call up a look, you dog'), then to rein it in, as Leontine goes to rhetorical extremes. Miss Richland is also acting, however, so the biter is well bit. She confounds Leontine by accepting him, knowing it is safe to do so because her well-informed maid has told her that Olivia is not Leontine's sister but his secret love. It is then that elopement becomes the only way out for Leontine and Olivia and the play moves into increasingly farcical regions.

Unsurprisingly, Mrs Bulkley enjoyed playing the lively, inven-tive Miss Richland, who gets so much fun from the deceits and confusions of others but whose steady affection for Honeywood is never in doubt. In the scene in Act IV when Honeywood flounders toward proposing (as it turns out, on behalf of Lofty), she goes as far as a well brought up eighteenth-century heroine could to offer him encouragement. She is not a Lady Betty, inhibited by delicacy from responding ardently to what she wants to hear. Yet she has fine feelings too. In fact, the actress had the best of both worlds, comic and sentimental.

The real acting problem was with Honeywood's part. The actor who created the role, Powell, thought it an impossible one: and modern actors have not been any more drawn to it, to judge from the paucity of revivals. Yet the play was important to Goldsmith, expressing as it did so much of his own experience. 'No man ever wrote so much from his feelings as Dr Goldsmith', said Reynolds. Around Honeywood feeling is confused, contradictory; a reflection, as suggested earlier, of how Goldsmith himself was viewed by many of his friends. The reviewer who found the play deficient in its 'fable' was surely right, though perhaps not in thinking the cure would be a fuller picture of Honeywood's 'distresses'. The nub of the problem for an actor is the difficulty of raising sympathy for a character who so often looks a weak, self-deceiving fool.

The difficulty is most acute in Act IV when Honeywood falls for Lofty's fulsome hints (obviously, as the audience can see, improvised on the spur of the moment) that he is the benefactor who has paid his debts and freed him from prison in his own home. Calling him 'thou best of men' – wildly inappropriate term for the slimy Lofty – he overdoes his gratitude grotesquely by consenting to propose to Miss Richland on his 'saviour's' behalf. Masochism of this order begins to look like a disease. In his soliloquy after Lofty's exit he does let slip some genuine feeling: 'And yet to see her in the possession of another! – Insupportable.' But he immediately overlays it with what he thinks he ought to feel.

In his defence it might be said that he is not the only one taken in by Lofty. The Croakers (and even Miss Richland for a time) are deceived by his offer to use his influence on the heiress' behalf. Mrs Croaker is impressed by his affected way of dragging his high-class friends into the conversation, as on his first entry in Act II when he calls to his servant, in a voice meant to be heard by the others, 'And if the Venetian Ambassador, or that teasing creature the Marquis, should call, I'm not at home', and then, to clinch the point: 'If the person calls about the commission, let him know that it is made out.' Contemporary reviewers did in fact query whether someone as well-to-do as Croaker would have been quite so easily gulled by such an 'arrogant pretender'. But the Croakers, after all, are broad, humorous characters whose reactions we are not meant to scrutinise as we do Honeywood's.

Miss Richland is another matter. Goldsmith takes care to have Sir William, that never-deceived judge, tell her in Act III that the 'important little man' who claims to be pressing her claim with Government is really 'quite contemptible among men in power'. She thus knows that he is a fraud before Honeywood shocks her with the proposal on his behalf: so her mortification is all the worse. She had defended Honeywood's 'tenderness, his humanity, his universal friendship' against Sir William's sterner view that men who pretend to 'universal benevolence' were either deceivers or dupes, who reasoned themselves into 'false feelings'. The vicarious proposal makes her change her mind. She leaves Honeywood on a sad parting line: 'I must disclaim his friendship who ceases to be a friend to himself.' Lofty being what he is, it is difficult to imagine Miss Richland's love for Honeywood surviving his crassness in proposing on the cheat's behalf. Goldsmith arranges a 'happy ending' for the lovers but he must have had his doubts about it. Certainly, when Garrick talked of reviving the play in 1773, Goldsmith announced that he would drop Lofty from the cast list, making the tantalisingly cryptic comment: he 'does not do'.

Has Honeywood's judgement been fatally disabled by his wish for 'universal benevolence'? This is the question that lurks in the play from the moment, at the start, when Sir William tells the old butler his plan to bring his nephew to his senses. Having already pretended to disinherit him, he now intends to 'involve him in fictitious distress, before he has plunged himself into real calamity. To arrest him for that very debt, to clap an officer upon him, and then let him see which of his friends will come to his relief.' The debate between the grieving supporters of the good-natured man in this scene extends the play into a philosophical dimension which has as much relevance for us today as it had for the eighteenth century. 'All the world loves him', says Jarvis, and Sir William: 'Say rather, that he loves all the world; that is his fault.' Honeywood has a good heart, says Jarvis, he keeps a place in it for the uncle he has not seen since he was a child. Sir William is not impressed: 'how can I be proud of a place in a heart where every sharper and coxcomb finds an easy entrance?' Is there a philosophic rationale to Honeywood's sentimental behaviour? Sir William refuses to grant any such authority:

> *Sir William*: My letters to him during my employment in Italy taught him only that philosophy which might prevent, not defend his errors.

Jarvis:	Faith, begging your honour's pardon. I'm sorry they taught him any philosophy at all; it has only serv'd to spoil him. This same philosophy is a good horse in the stable, but an errant jade on a journey. For my own part, whenever I hear him mention the name on't, I'm always sure he's going to play the fool.
Sir William:	Don't let us ascribe his faults to his philosophy, I entreat you. No, Jarvis, his good nature arises rather from his fears of offending the importunate, than his desire of making the deserving happy.
Jarvis:	What it rises from, I don't know. But, to be sure, everybody has it that asks it.

(I.20)

In some ways, as we have seen, *The Good Natur'd Man* is firmly tied to its own time. Audiences who came to Goldsmith's first night on 29 January 1768, would have felt in a familiar world. While Mrs Harley, on the Drury Lane stage, was expressing her mixed feelings about Lady Betty's sensibility – 'And yet somehow, foolish as it is, one can't help liking it' – Jarvis was doing much the same for Honeywood at Covent Garden: 'the strange, good-natur'd, foolish, open-hearted – And yet, all his faults are such that one loves him still the better for them.' They would have recognised Honeywood as a typical young man of his time in some respects, idiosyncratic as he is in others. He has an upper-class disdain (to be seen again in Charles Surface) for paying bills. Tradesmen and moneylenders don't count. When Jarvis pleads for the 'little broker in Crooked-lane' who 'says he has been at a great deal of trouble to get back the money you borrowed', Honeywood dismisses him with a joke: 'That I don't know; but I'm sure we were at a great deal of trouble in getting him to lend it.' 'There's that ten guineas', says Jarvis, 'you were sending to the poor gentleman and his children in the Fleet. I believe that would stop his mouth, for a while at least.' 'Ay, Jarvis', is the cool reply 'but what will fill their mouths in the meantime? Must I be cruel because he happens to be importunate; and, to relieve his avarice, leave them in insupportable distress?'

Yet there are issues in the play which we can recognise, perhaps with a slight shock, as very much alive today. We have our own word, 'wet' to describe liberally-minded as opposed to 'hard line' politicians. The term suggests just the same ambivalence in people's attitudes to liberalism now as in Goldsmith's play. Honeywood is a 'wet' of the first water, we might say. The term takes in the good as well as the excessive in his behaviour. His insolvency is caused by his charitableness as much as by his love of fine clothes (such as the blue and gold suit lent to the bailiff). He has a modern sensibility about some things, as for instance in shrinking from the idea of prosecuting the servant caught stealing plate. Jarvis would like to see him 'turn'd off at Tyburn', a nasty reminder of the fate a thief could expect. Honeywood, more humanely, will not add to the loss of the plate 'the loss of a fellow creature'. He is remarkably patient with his drunken butler – though for Jarvis this is no virtue but a sloppy laissez faire style of management which has resulted in his employing 'a pack of drunken servants'.

Finally, it seems that Honeywood's ability to enjoy the rough vitality of 'low' characters like the servants and the bailiffs is the most sympathetic feature of his character. It was surely a trait that endeared him to his creator. Through the odd, interesting, maddening, character of this sentimental hero Goldsmith made a breach in the polite edifice of eighteenth-century comedy. It was to be smashed wide open in his next play, when the rustic Dionysus, Tony Lumpkin, pushed his way from the public house to centre stage and that modern-minded heroine, Kate Hardcastle, took advantage of his subversive joke to 'conquer' all restrictions on her. It is understandable that *The Good Natur'd Man* has attracted less attention than its brilliant successor but still, it is a play with something for our time. A sharp modern production might be able to point up the 'fable' and bring the oddity of Honeywood's behaviour – the dilemma of sentimentalism – to the fore. Perhaps the play could even be seen as contributing to the great discussion about social virtues and vices which plays such as David Hare's *Racing Demon* (1990) keep going in our theatre, as the sentimental comedy did in Goldsmith's.

By the time Sheridan came on the scene sentimental comedy was no longer the threat it had seemed to Goldsmith – largely as a result of what Goldsmith had done to counter it. Perhaps more as a jovial tribute to his predecessor than in burning zeal Sheridan picked up the old cudgels in his second prologue to *The Rivals*, where he poured scorn on the Sentimental Muse. The prologue must have suited the sprightly Mrs Bulkley for it is really more taken up with the actors and their mannerisms than with philosophic questions about the nature of comedy. She would find it amusing, when pointing to the effigy representing the Muse of Comedy, to echo Tom King's lines from *False Delicacy* with mock indignation: 'Look on her well – does she seem form'd to teach?/ Should you expect to hear this lady – preach?' The satire is not to be taken too seriously, her merry style seems to suggest. The Sentimental Muse is 'too chaste to look like flesh and blood', she says, and the audience must agree; after all, she is only 'primly portray'd on emblematic wood'. The audience are invited to enjoy the fun of imagining the Covent Garden company totally miscast, to suit the sentimental mode, their best loved comedians forced into seriousness; Harry Woodward made to 'knock Ned Shuter down' instead of fool with him. The prologue is recognisably by the author of *The Critic*, already at the start of his career fascinated by what could be done with actors and theatre conventions.

In his own comedies, Sheridan's attitude to sentiment was no less complex than Goldsmith's, as we will see. In his adaptation of *The Relapse*, on the other hand, his approach was straightforward and business-like. If Vanbrugh's play were to be shown at all, it had to be 'refined'; Sheridan simply set about doing it as artfully as possible. Amusingly, for a playwright so prone himself to write at too great length, he made it his task to tighten up Vanbrugh's loosely constructed plot and did achieve a new unity by setting the whole action in Scarborough instead of part in London, part in Sir Tunbelly's house in the country. Much of his ruthless cutting is in aid of this neater, tighter plot. He made the hilarious episode of Lord Foppington's attempt to prove he is himself and his brother an impostor lead straight into the finale while the theatrical temperature was still at its highest point. Vanbrugh indulged in further complications by having Miss Hoyden determine (after she has discovered that Young Fashion has cheated her into marriage) to marry for a second time and achieve her 'Lord' after all. Vanbrugh evidently relished the opportunity for some additional satire afforded by the would-be bigamy, as when the corrupt chaplain argues that if committed in the right spirit, it is 'no more than to be drunk by way of physic'.

Sheridan chose to cut the play off before it moves into these murky waters. He would probably have preferred to do so even if the Hoyden remarrying episode had not threatened offence to his squeamish audience (Dr Bull, the Nurse and the insatiable Miss Hoyden become increasingly coarse fare in Vanbrugh's fifth act). There is a sense of a 'natural' climax to the farcical plot at the end of the long drawn out masquerade which ends in the revelation that Miss Hoyden has been married secretly to Young Fashion, passing himself off as her intended husband, Lord Foppington. Most of the time, one suspects, Sheridan's instinct for a clear-cut shape in comedy helped him to perform his amputations without too much agonising. Not all his cuts were dictated by his audience's prudish taste. They might indeed have felt quite at home with Act I scene i which consists of a sickly conversation between Loveless and Amanda in deplorable blank verse on the virtuous joys of marriage and the forthcoming 'fiery trial of my virtue', as Loveless puts it (represented by a winter to be spent in dangerous London). In 1777 the scene was no longer the piquant sequel it had been to theatre-goers of 1696, fresh from seeing Loveless reformed by Amanda in *Love's Last Shift*. In cutting the scene Sheridan may have been amused to recognise that Vanbrugh in sentimental vein was just as mawkish as any sentimentalist of his own day, if anything rather below eighteenth-century standard.

Other cuts and bowdlerisings must have troubled him somewhat more. Vanbrugh's dashing young widow, Berinthia, had to lose some of her wittiest lines. It was no longer possible for her to give Amanda quite such frank lessons in the way of the world or to entertain the audience with saucy jokes like her *sotto voce* comment, when Amanda remarks on the improvement in her friend since her marriage and widowhood: 'Alack a-day, there has gone more than that to improve me, if she knew all!' Her realistic view of sex and marriage had to be censored. On Sheridan's stage she did not tell Amanda that her reason for marrying a man she detested was that otherwise 'my mother would have whipped me'. Nor did she hint that marriage was by no means the best way to sexual pleasure: 'If you'll consult the widows of this town, they'll tell you you should never take a lease of a house you can hire for a quarter's warning.' She could remain lively on Sheridan's stage only so far as would fit with her being an 'innocent', as she claims to be and the audience needed to believe.

Sheridan was said to have blamed himself, in conversation, for spoiling Vanbrugh's play and in *The Critic* he certainly makes fun of the sort of bowdlerising he had performed. When Sneer and Mrs Dangle lament the changes which threaten 'the true sentimental' (which has 'nothing ridiculous in it from the beginning to the end') Dangle sharply corrects them. The worst change is in the debilitating 'nicety of the audience': 'No double entendre, no smart innuendo admitted; even Vanbrugh and Congreve obliged to undergo a bungling reformation.' Sheridan takes off into regions of pure absurdity here, anticipating the world of *The Importance of Being Earnest* when Sneer makes his sublime remark on the need for earnestness: 'the theatre in proper hands might certainly be made the school of morality, but now, I am sorry to say it, people seem to go there principally for their entertainment!'

Could Sheridan really have wished away a phenomenon that stimulated his wit so superbly? Hardly. The impression created by the plays (whatever he said outside them) is his sheer delight in the absurdities of the sentimentalists. No doubt he winced a little when he cut some of Vanbrugh's wittiest lines. It was axiomatic, however, that frank sex talk and bawdy jokes would have to go. The fun he has with the whole idea of 'reformation' in *The Critic* makes it more than likely that he got some saturnine amusement out of the exercise of reforming *The Relapse.* He can be imagined rattling through Vanbrugh's play, picking up phrases or incidents likely to offend, and enjoying the challenge of finding ingenious ways round them. Some changes could be made by simple cuts, as with Lord Foppington's bold aside (made under the husband's nose): 'I mean to lie with your wife.' Some little verbal changes reflect the move away from physical brutality in the treatment of women. Miss Hoyden, for instance, no longer says that she will put on her laced smock to meet her intended husband 'though I'm whipped till the blood run down my heels for't'. Now the imagined punishment is to be 'lock'd up a month for 't'.

Some changes were more radical. Sheridan must have been pleased with himself when he solved the problem of retaining, for the sake of the plot, a character who would have petrified his audience, the blatantly homosexual Coupler, who helps Young Fashion to the heiress. His solution was simply to change the sex and make 'Madam' Coupler more avaricious for money than for the 'warm body' which is the reward Vanbrugh's Young Fashion agrees to bestow on his 'old Satan' ('take possession as soon as thou wilt').

Sheridan could not allow Berinthia to have a full-blown affair with Loveless; nor could he go quite as far as Vanbrugh with the threatened rape of Amanda by Worthy (the last character being replaced by the rather more sentimental Townly). It may be, as critics have tended to agree, that the result of all this sexual restraint is a too bland comedy. Yet Sheridan found a method congenial to him in keeping the lovers poised just this side of the 'sentimental' danger line. Rather than individual and private, the assignations in his version are public; a matter of crossed lines, overheard conversations, gaily improbable coincidences through which each separate pair comes to realise the truth about the feelings of the other. The encounters and eavesdroppings in the moonlit garden of Act V are deftly orchestrated, in the way of an operatic quartet; the great quartet at the climax of *The Marriage of Figaro* comes to mind. As so often with Sheridan, comic opera provides a clue to the convention he works in with most ease and pleasure. From that point of view *A Trip to Scarborough*, though not to be compared for wit with *The Relapse*, has its own validity. Sheridan was no more than Goldsmith depressed by the sentimental mode. It fed their drama, as fuel for their satire and in other incalculable ways.

5
'She Stoops to Conquer'

She Stoops to Conquer is both perfectly theatrical and perfectly natural. This is the effect which charmed its first audience and has helped the play to hold the stage ever since. It proclaims itself as a piece of theatre at the start when the prologue plunges into a specialised battle, Goldsmith's vendetta against 'the mawkish drab of spurious breed,/ Who deals in *sentimentals*'. Modern audiences seldom hear this in-joke, productions nowadays tending to cut the prologue. But there are plenty of sly allusions inside the play to theatre matters, either explicit or to be deduced: jokes about the audience's horror of the 'low' and Kate's enquiry to her maid whether she looks 'something like Cherry in *The Beaux' Stratagem?*' The characters' thoughts run naturally to play-acting. It is enough for her maid to tell her that Marlow mistook her mistress for a barmaid to inspire Kate with an instant resolve to play the part. The audience attending Goldsmith's play is called on to have the same alertness as Kate to acting possibilities. From one angle, the play is to be seen as a gigantic histrionic joke, one mistake growing out of another and feeding new roles, as in that most theatrical of forms, the *commedia dell'arte*.

We can feel this theatrical impulse at work – in Kate's changes of role, in Tony's comic inventions – even if it is harder for us than for the original audience to recognise the specific theatrical sources on which Goldsmith drew (whether consciously or otherwise). Isaac Bickerstaffe's comic opera, *Love in a Village*, was one such (it had appeared in 1762, so characters like Hodge, the country bumpkin, sometimes seen as a prototype for Tony Lumpkin, must have been still fresh in the minds of Goldsmith's audience). Behind that was Marivaux' *Le Jeu de l'amour et du hasard*, which, as we saw, anticipated the idea of upper-class lovers playing servants in order to test each other's character. Anyone familiar with *She Stoops to Conquer* only as a text needs to imagine the difference staging would make to some of its unlikelier incidents. Marlow's failure to recognise Kate after their first meeting is both funnier and more convincing when we have shared his view of the well wrapped-up Miss Hardcastle in her outdoor dress, her face shaded by a bonnet, and seen him (as in Tom Courtenay's neurotic interpretation) so self-conscious that he scarcely dare raise his eyes to get a closer look at her. The point is made in the text ('he never once looked up during the interview', III.i) but it is more effective when acted out. Stage illusion is still more important in Tony's third practical joke, when he takes his mother on the 'dangerous' journey which goes round in a circle and lands her in her own garden. The audience know she is being gulled, but if they are to feel the force of her panic (as one should, in farce) they too must share a little in the impression of an unknown, threatening world of quagmires and highwaymen which Tony conjures up out of the most ordinary materials – the essence of stage illusion. In the National Theatre's 1984 production a large overhanging tree, atmospherically lit, conveyed an effect appropriate both to the real place the characters are in, the garden, and Crack-skull Common where they think they are.

Goldsmith unusually combines all this extrovert histrionic juggling in the *commedia* convention with a more inward view of character (such as John Loftis has rightly attributed to sentimental comedy). He achieves acute psychological revelations, often of an intensely personal kind, without sacrificing the bold comic form in which he was most at ease on the stage. Perhaps to be outrageously comic was the only way he could be utterly natural. John Ginger has suggested that his most aggressively comic character, Tony Lumpkin, was a projection from deep psychic regions and reflected Goldsmith's troubled relationship with his mother, his need for release of a dionysiac 'Hodge' within himself. More obviously, Marlow's double nature, as already suggested, must have some reference to Goldsmith's social awkwardness, perhaps also to his sexual inhibitions. That last is speculative, but it is always clear when the part is sensitively played that psychological knots of a very real kind need to be unknotted before this divided young man can be sexually at ease with himself.

The plot is immensely contrived, as befits a farce, which the play partly is. Horace Walpole thought it was nothing but that: 'Dr Goldsmith has written a comedy – no, it is the lowest of all farces.'[1] He was wrong in categorising it so narrowly. But he correctly identified an important structural principle, the regard for tightness and speed which separates farce from more loosely constructed comedy. Goldsmith takes pains to keep his plot line bold and clear, giving the audience something to hold on to when the action moves into its more manic phases. Nothing is admitted that does not work on the farcical level. Tony Lumpkin ensures that even the secondary lovers' plot, potentially a tamer affair, leads into explosions of comic chaos.

Remarkably, however, this contrived plot which continually draws attention to its own theatricality, is infused with naturalness and realism at every point. Take the revealing little episode with the 'awkward' servants, Diggory and company, at the start of Act II. It follows fast (only seconds in stage time) on the scene showing Marlow and Hastings leaving the Three Pigeons for the 'Buck's Head' and ends as they arrive. The speed is necessary in farcical terms: we must not be given too long to reflect on the fantastic mistake. But it is also near enough to 'real' time (we were told that it was a short journey from the Three Pigeons) to preserve an impression of naturalness. Mr Hardcastle's attempt at training his servants is germane to the plot: the country-bumpkin ways of Diggory and the rest fit Marlow's idea of what can be expected from a shabby country inn, hence he continues in his mistake. Yet the un-smart servants are also entirely natural, given Mr Hardcastle's character and his passionate devotion to old country ways. He does not really expect to train his servants to high standards, we can see, but is simply setting up a performance for Marlow's benefit; one that is almost bound to fail. Amused exasperation is the sternest note he strikes when issuing warnings they should not need: not to keep their hands in their pockets when addressed by guests, not to pop out to stare at visitors 'and then run in again, like frighted rabbits'; not to join in with the laughter at some funny story when they wait at table. Diggory, taken from the barn for the new job, knows his master will be easily persuaded to relax his embargoes:

Diggory:　　　Then, ecod, your worship must not tell the story of

> Ould Grouse in the gun-room: I can't help laughing
> at that – he! he! he! – for the soul of me. We have
> laughed at that these twenty years. – ha! ha! ha!
>
> *Hardcastle*: Ha! ha! ha! The story is a good one. Well, honest
> Diggory, you may laugh at that – but still remem-
> ber to be attentive.
>
> (II.i.35)

There is a whole world of reality here. It has a touch of the rustic
freedom which the Greeks allowed on to their stage in the satyr
plays performed as 'afterpieces' to their tragedies, to use the
eighteenth-century term for the curious arrangement. Tony Harri-
son's *Trackers* (1989), which incorporated in a modern framework
the only fragment extant of a satyr play by Sophocles, argued
rumbustiously that the uninhibited song and dance of the satyrs
had been deliberately degraded and repressed by the high, élitist
art of Apollo and his followers. It is an argument Goldsmith would
have understood. His satyrs are more restrained but he makes a
bolder demand for their place on the English stage; not in an
'afterpiece' but right at the centre,[2] especially when Tony Lumpkin is in the ascendant. The confusion in which the training scene
breaks up, with the servants already forgetting their orders and
'running about, as if frighted, different ways' hints at the wildness
inherent in satyr comedy. It is also a paradigm of the farcical chaos
that will engulf master, mistress and guests later in the play. The
scene is a little jewel, setting a crucial note of sympathy with the
country view of things at the same time as feeding a plot which
depends on the townsfolk taking a less sympathetic view.

The plot points established in Act I all demonstrate the double
aspect in which the action is to be viewed. Familiar theatrical
conventions such as the Restoration opposition of town and
country are infused with new human feeling. Mrs Hardcastle is in a
long line of characters who hanker after town delights and squab-
ble with husbands who withhold them. Goldsmith gets fun out of
this clash of wills, as Congreve and Wycherley had before him. But
he humanises it when Mr Hardcastle responds to his wife's complaint about the 'old-fashioned trumpery' in their way of life with
gentle humour: 'And I love it. I love everything that's old; old
friends, old times, old manners, old books, old wine; and I believe, Dorothy (*Taking her hand*), you'll own I have been pretty

fond of an old wife.' The sentiment is real, we may believe; though Mrs Hardcastle vigorously rejects it, cross at being described as 'old': 'I promise you, I'm not so old as you'd make me, by more than one good year. Add twenty to twenty, and make money of that.'

Her vanity about her age operates on various levels. It is very funny, as in the scene (II.i) when Hastings flatters her on her youthful looks, telling her that fifty is likely to be the most fashionable age for ladies in the next London season. 'Then I shall be too young for the fashion!', she remarks complacently. This is an absurdity to be savoured, yet the ludicrous vanity also requires to be taken a little more seriously. She goes very far in her determination to sustain her own fictions and to achieve her aim of marrying Tony to Constance and of holding on to the latter's jewels as long as possible. There is a hint of obsession in her riposte to Constance's demand for her property: 'It will be time enough for jewels, my dear, twenty years hence, when your beauty begins to want repairs.' Her son identifies something clamourous and lawless in her when, in answer to her complaint that he never delights her with his 'agreeable, wild notes', he says, 'Ecod! Mama, your own notes are the wildest of the two'.

Much of the plot turns on Mrs Hardcastle's unreliability on questions of age. When she asserts that she is still quite young ('Add twenty to twenty and make money of that') and her husband good-humouredly corrects her – 'Let me see; twenty added to twenty, makes just fifty and seven' – she 'proves' that she is right by referring to Tony's birth: 'I was but twenty when I was brought to bed of Tony, that I had by Mr Lumpkin, my first husband; and he's not come to years of discretion yet.' Can we believe her? Doubt is sown, although it is not till the end of the play, literally its last minutes, that Mr Hardcastle reveals the well-kept secret to Tony: 'I must now declare, you have been of age these last three months.' The audience knows by then just what power Mrs Hardcastle gained by letting her son think he was still legally a minor, and what selfish uses she put it to. It is a further black mark against her.

Goldsmith's delicate art, however, does not permit him to make Mrs Hardcastle purely a figure of fun, a kind of maternal monster. To play her as he wrote her, an actress would need to register, as well as her absurdities, the violence of her feelings as she swings between infatuation with her son ('my charmer', 'lovey', 'poor boy') and fury at his failure of response. A modern feminist interpretation would also invite sympathy for her resentment at her narrow social life. Mr Hardcastle sees her craving for fashion simply as female weakness, echoing, though less nastily, those many misogynists on the English stage before him who enjoyed railing at women's love of clothes. We can hardly be expected to agree with him; any more, surely, than did his author (so known for his extravagance on finery). Mrs Hardcastle was portrayed as much younger than is usual in the 1989 performance at the Royal Exchange Theatre, Manchester, an interesting move which could have added a layer of psychological interest, though in fact the production aimed more at farce. It is understandable: we cannot but laugh at the more absurd aspects of the love-hate relationship between mother and son. Tony's mirth in his wicked tricks is infectious and we are free to revel in them because he is so often the agent of a kind of comic nemesis. When he torments his mother (III.i) by chanting with gusto, 'I can bear witness to that', her rage is a kind of punishment for her willingness to deceive Constance by pretending that her jewels have been stolen. But the farce should not be played too hard, for there is also some subtle psychology in the scene. It is very revealing that the terms of abuse she hurls at her son express just the sort of contempt her husband has for him, and which she normally repudiates indignantly. 'Booby', she calls him, and 'blockhead', 'cross-grained brute'; more wounding, unexpected terms from her than the 'viper' or 'provoking, undutiful boy' that she has hurled in temper, in earlier scenes.

Her emotional state is in fact treated with far more psychological exactitude than is common in farce, presenting actors and directors with some testing choices of emphasis. The same is true of the great practical joke itself. Behind it lies a deep family rift. When Mrs Hardcastle remarks in the opening dialogue that Tony has 'not come to years of discretion yet', 'discretion' refers to the age of legal majority. Mr Hardcastle takes it in a different sense; there is real bitterness in his quip. 'Nor ever will, I dare answer for him'. The gulf between husband and wife has a source, we can see, in the behaviour of this offspring who only half belongs; the stepson, child of the long-dead Lumpkin, the misfit, more at ease in the public house than in the house which will one day be his own. For he, not sensible Kate, beloved of her father, is the heir to

the estate, as his drinking companions recognise when they call
him 'Squire'. Goldsmith uses some effective visual symbolism to
reinforce this view of Tony as someone who does not quite belong
in his own home. On his first appearance the stage direction
emphasises that he is merely '*crossing the Stage*' (en route for the
Three Pigeons). He resists his mother's entreaty to stay, to the
extent of having a physical battle with her; a real tug of war:

Mrs Hardcastle:	You shan't go.
Tony:	I will, I tell you.
Mrs Hardcastle:	I say you shan't.
Tony:	We'll see which is strongest, you or I.
	(I.i.80)

Their undignified exit, he 'hauling her out' is a good comic symbol
of the more inward battle going on between them throughout the
play; he seeking to assert his independence, she trying to keep him
the 'spoilt' boy she has made him by her alternate cossetting and
scolding. She has been 'dosing' him ever since he was born, he tells
her later in the play (II), and snubbing him when he is in spirits: 'If
I'm to have any good, let it come of itself; not to keep dinging it,
dinging it into one so.'

This is stuff that would serve for a realistic modern drama.
Throughout the play a strong vein of psychological interest accompanies the broader comedy. Symbolic focal points appear.
Well before the stage scene switches to the Three Pigeons in Act I,
we are made to feel the curious force of the place: each character
(except Kate) is placed in relation to that magnetic centre. Mrs
Hardcastle envisages the society there – a 'low, paltry set of
fellows' – as if they really were an anonymous chorus of satyrs,
while Tony rather touchingly insists on their individualism. The
low fellows, for him, have names and occupations: Dick Muggins
the exciseman, Jack Slang, the horse doctor. Mr Hardcastle, despite his love of country ways, follows his wife's line in deploring
the company Tony keeps. Tom Baker's interpretation of the role
in the 1984 production at the National Theatre hinted at some
tension in the character between his bonhomie and his social
prejudices. He makes friends of his 'booby' servants but cannot
stand the idea of his wife's son bringing booby ways into the
drawing room.

The great practical joke has powerful drives behind it, some below the level of conscious articulation. Tony's iconoclastic enjoyment in playing tricks is a starting point, as Goldsmith establishes by having Mr Hardcastle complain in the first scene about schoolboyish pranks, like tying his stepfather's wig to the back of his chair. The inveterate practical joker would naturally take the chance of having fun with the lost travellers at the Three Pigeons. Tony Haygarth's Lumpkin made this sense of fun a chief trait in the character. His high animal spirits were demonstrated in a very physical way as he hauled his mother about in I.i or played noisily on a bugle, amusingly illustrating his stepfather's account of him as a 'speaking trumpet'. When he hit on his master joke, enjoyment in his own quick-witted fancies was as strong a drive as a wish for revenge on the 'old grumbletonian' who has been 'calling me whelp, and hound, this half-year'. Haygarth's Tony built on the suggestion of jocular half-affection in the expression, 'old grumbletonian'. Exasperation rather than deep-seated bitterness was the driving motive here: it was a revenge but a comic one, harming no one (in fact, it can be seen as doing everyone good in the end). Audiences have always felt affection for Tony even though he represents an anarchic force which could at any point have had more disastrous consequences. Always in the background, after all, is the thought of how badly he has been brought up by a mother who thinks all the learning her son needs is his 'fifteen hundred a year'. At a deeper psychic level still, there is a suggestion of dionysiac glee at upsetting an established order uncongenial to the youth who hankers after Bet Bouncer, with her cheeks as red as pulpit cushions and ranks his 'low' friends above his prospective brother-in-law. 'Gentlemen', he says to Dick and the rest, when preparing to meet Marlow and Hastings, 'as they mayn't be good enough company for you, step down for a moment and I'll be with you in the squeezing of a lemon.'

Tony proves decisively that he is no booby in this scene. The joke succeeds in the first place because he understands character and accurately gauges his victims' likely reactions to the disconcerting situation devised for them. He knows just what traits of Mr Hardcastle will fit in with the idea of an innkeeper who 'wants to be thought a gentleman' and can deduce the effect their host's apparent pushiness will have on Marlow and Hastings from observing their haughty ways and Marlow's deep reserve.

According to Hastings, they lost their way because Marlow was too reserved to ask for directions.) Tony is provided with another revenge motive when Marlow unwittingly insults him by quoting what gossip says, that he is 'an awkward booby, reared up and spoilt at his mother's apron-string'. Much of the comic pleasure of Act II comes from seeing Mr Hardcastle, Marlow and Hastings behave exactly as Tony's scenario would have it. Hastings does indeed quote from the joker's script at one point, when Mr Hardcastle starts talking about 'my uncle, Colonel Wallop': 'His uncle a colonel!', mutters Hastings, and then, echoing Tony's joke: 'we shall soon hear of his mother being a Justice of Peace.'

The cream of the joke is that it gives both parties totally reasonable grounds for irritation; Mr Hardcastle for being snubbed and the young men for being continually interrupted, as in their attempt to discuss what clothes they will wear when they meet their girls (luck enters here; had they named names, the trick would have come out):

Marlow: We approve your caution and hospitality, sir. (*To Hastings*) I have been thinking, George, of changing our travelling dresses in the morning. I am grown confoundedly ashamed of mine.

Hardcastle: I beg, Mr Marlow, you'll use no ceremony in this house.

Hastings: I fancy, Charles, you're right: the first blow is half the battle. I intend opening the campaign with the white and gold.

Hardcastle: Mr Marlow – Mr Hastings – gentlemen – pray be under no constraint in this house. This is Liberty-Hall, gentlemen. You may do just as you please here.

Marlow: Yet George, if we open the campaign too fiercely at first, we may want ammunition before it is over. I think to reserve the embroidery to secure a retreat.

Hardcastle: Your talking of a retreat, Mr Marlow, puts me in mind of the Duke of Marlborough, when we went to besiege Denain . . .

(II.i.152)

Sympathy is more or less evenly divided in the scene, as it might be in the real-life situation it reflects. Why should travellers listen to a landlord's tedious reminiscences of ill-remembered campaigns (the dates are all wrong, critics have noted) when they need a glass of punch and a menu? And why should Hardcastle put up with the extraordinary rudeness of the young men he is receiving as guests? Each is so right while being so wrong: reason is stood on its head, as in all anarchical, dionysiac comedy. Yet we do not altogether part company with the rational world. We are always aware of the individual characteristics that keep the mistake going. Despite all the provocation, Hardcastle is sufficiently imbued with old-fashioned notions of hospitality to offer Marlow a cup, prepared 'with my own hands', asking him to pledge 'to our better acquaintance'. Marlow softens: 'A very impudent fellow this! but he's a character, and I'll humour him a little. Sir, my service to you.' The excellence of the cup produces further softening: addressing Hardcastle as 'my old friend', he enquires about his business: 'Warm work, now and then, at elections, I suppose.' Perhaps credulity is strained when Hardcastle uses a rather too patly misleading proverbial phrase in describing his electoral position: 'Since our betters have hit upon the expedient of electing each other, there's no business for us that sell ale.' But the turn of phrase is not inconsistent with his love of everything countrified and old-fashioned. He behaves naturally, as do the young men in calling peremptorily for the menu, and being very rude about it: 'Damn your pig's face, I say', 'And damn your prune sauce, say I'.

The mood swings to and fro, never turning quite so sour that eventual reconciliation would seem too unlikely. The delicate balance that is called for between farce and comedy of character was achieved in the NT production of 1984. A fundamentally good-natured tone was maintained even in scenes where bafflement is on the verge of the surreal, as when Marlow goes off, 'to see that our beds are aired, and properly taken care of' while Hardcastle protests, 'I entreat you'll leave all that to me'. The aside comes into its own here, allowing the civilities, however strained, to continue, while the irritation is expressed *sotto voce*:

Marlow: You see I'm resolved on it. (*Aside*) A very troublesome fellow this, as ever I met with.

Hardcastle: Well sir, I'm resolved at least to attend you.
(*Aside*) This may be modern modesty, but I never saw anything look so like old-fashioned impudence.

(II.i.302)

Tony's trick might have been expected to come to a halt when Hastings meets Constance and she enlightens him: 'An inn! sure you mistake! my aunt, my guardian lives here. What could induce you to think this house an inn?' But, again, traits of character determine the outcome. Hastings reacts opportunistically. In order to have more time with Constance to finalise plans for their elopement, he is prepared to keep the truth from his friend. Otherwise, he tells Constance, they would have to leave the house at once, because the 'strange reserve' of Marlow's temper would demand it. Not so very strange, we might say. This is a moment when sympathy begins to flow to Marlow, now being cheated not only by Tony Lumpkin but by his closest friend. Marlow is bitter about it when he learns the truth. The 'booby' he can forgive, but how could his friend deliberately leave him in such a humiliating mistake, let him be 'Rendered contemptible, driven into ill manners, despised, insulted, laughed at'.

That the upshot is not just humiliation is due to the intervention of a very determined character, one who is seeking personal satisfaction, but who in the process brings near-miraculous release from his neurosis to Marlow. For Kate, as for Hastings and Constance, the great mistake is a way to sexual freedom; in her case, freedom to find out whether or not she wants to marry the man intended for her husband. Mr Hardcastle's house becomes in a deep sense the 'Liberty-Hall' he conventionally invited Marlow and Hastings to make it. Tony Lumpkin, like a satyr king, has set in motion a free-wheeling vehicle on to which the young people scramble, Kate in the suitably dionysiac disguise of a barmaid.

When Goldsmith changed the title from 'The Mistakes of a Night' to *She Stoops to Conquer* he seized on something central and special in his play. The original title had its own appropriateness, hinting at the farce in the plot and also at its 'sentimental' interest in the mistakes people make about each other. But the new title – surfacing just at the last, in the way of inspired inventions – identified the heart of the play, not as 'mistake' but as 'will' and 'choice'. It is the advantage Kate Hardcastle takes of Marlow's mistake that drives the main action from the moment she discovers it.

In the lively character of Kate, Goldsmith created the one theatre heroine of the century capable of joining the company of spirited girls – Rosalind, Viola, Millamant – who have charmed audiences with their witty resourcefulness in shaping their own marriage fortunes. Like Rosalind, she puts on a disguise which allows her to teach her man how best to woo her: she is called on for more artifice than anyone in the play except her half-brother (they have more in common than one might think). Yet she is also perfectly natural. Wit and nature combine to cast a bright glow over her first scene with her father when he 'sells' Marlow to her:

Hardcastle:	I am told he's a man of an excellent understanding.
Miss Hardcastle:	Is he?
Hardcastle:	Very generous.
Miss Hardcastle:	I believe I shall like him.
Hardcastle:	Young and brave.
Miss Hardcastle:	I'm sure I shall like him.
Hardcastle:	And very handsome.
Miss Hardcastle:	My dear papa, say no more (*Kissing his hand*), he's mine, I'll have him.

(I.i.118)

The stiff conventions of the sentimental comedy are invested with human vitality in the lively scene. This is a father/daughter relationship with a relaxed modern note, despite eighteenth-century gestures like hand-kissing. The audience sees at the start there is an affectionate understanding between father and daughter. She intends to have her own way but she respects him and humours his foibles: about her clothes and, more serious, his obsession with old friends which makes him so set on her marrying the son of Sir Charles Marlow. He in his turn clearly dotes on 'his pretty darling Kate', and would probably not force her to marry against her will, though this is never tested.

Kate's assurance and ease in social relations, due partly, no doubt, to her good relationship with her father (we never see her with her so-different mother) are the key which unlocks Marlow's blocked personality. How has he become the 'singular character' described by Constance in Act I.i: 'Among women of reputation and virtue he is the modestest man alive; but his acquaintance give him a very different character among creatures of another stamp: you understand me' Goldsmith supplies no other answer than Marlow's own analysis of his trouble. As the friends chat in Act II. i, Hastings puts the crucial question: how is it that a travelled young man like his friend, with his 'opportunities' and 'natural good sense', so lacks assurance? Tom Courtenay's Marlow struck a note of ironic humour in his dry reply, 'The Englishman's malady', but then went on with some passion to recall the education that has left him such a divided personality: life 'chiefly spent in a college, or an inn, in seclusion from that lovely part of the creation that chiefly teach men confidence.' Already, before he meets Kate, there is a suggestion that all he needs is someone like her, if only he can be got to overcome his ambiguous 'modesty'.

Tony's trick provides the means and Kate's vivacious intelligence does the rest. Like her predecessor, Miss Richland, she gets some fun out of her lover's agonies of embarrassment. When he meets 'Miss Hardcastle' she makes him writhe, finishing off his tortuous phrases for him and interpreting his mumbled attempts at sentimental truisms. The rhetoric of sentimentalism is dealt a hard blow in her sharp account (III.i) of the 'sober sentimental interview'. 'He treated me with diffidence and respect; censured the manners of the age; admired the prudence of girls that never laughed.'

The scene makes Marlow absurd – but it also helps to move sympathy toward him: he suffers during the intolerable 'interview' and has to be seen in a more kindly light. If he is beginning to reveal himself, she too is releasing a part of her real personality. There is truth behind the performance: the merry, teasing side already seen in the first-act conversation with her father, finds in the barmaid role opportunities not open to 'Miss Hardcastle'. Again like her brother, though with vastly more finesse, she enters the world of the 'low' in order to find freedom to be herself.

It is the sense that she is feeling her way to self-expression as well as testing Marlow that keeps her masquerade from seeming a rather cruel, if amusing game. When she forces him to look at her, drawing him from studious immersion in his 'tablets' with her repeated 'Did you call, sir?' (III.i) she is relying on the amorous response she gets. Marlow dances to her tune from the moment he declares, 'I vow, child, you are vastly handsome' and tries to kiss her. He notes her 'sprightly, malicious eye' and momentarily suspects some malice in her when she laughs a little too heartily at his account of being a favourite with the ladies, 'their agreeable Rattle'. 'Egad' he mutters in one of the asides that form a crucial counterpoint to the 'heard' dialogue: 'I don't quite like this chit. She looks knowing, methinks.' She has already led him on to talk about 'Miss Hardcastle', complaining that he addresses her in a very different manner: 'you looked dashed, and kept bowing to the ground'. His derogatory remarks about the cool young lady who reduced him to such a jelly lay up humiliations for him when the truth comes out in Act V. Kate does not scruple to rub salt in the wound, reminding him how he described himself as a ladies' man and 'Miss Hardcastle' as an 'awkward, squinting thing'.

But by the time she twits him with these embarrassments, we know they were necessary to his therapy: he had to reveal all his inadequacies and vanities before he could be fully himself with her. Similarly, she now knows her own mind; that, despite his failings, he is the man for her. As she assures her father when he surprises her in a lover-like struggle with Marlow: 'He has only the faults that will pass off with time, and the virtues that will improve with age.' Boldly, given his prudish audience, Goldsmith allows her to respond with sophistication to Marlow's amorous overtures. She obviously gets pleasure from leading him on and remains amused and saucy when refusing his proposal to visit her room, to examine her 'embroidery': 'Ay, but the colours don't look well by candlelight.' Modern actors could be forgiven for reading more into this than Goldsmith would have intended, but for him, as certainly for his original audience, Kate was unquestionably virtuous and Marlow, once he believed that, would not think of trying to seduce her, even though he is on fire for the 'tempting, brisk, lovely little thing that runs about the house with a bunch of keys to its girdle'.

A triple sexual revolt is triumphantly carried through in *She Stoops to Conquer*, by the power of wit and play-acting. Of the three sets of lovers (we may think of Bet Bouncer as Tony's off-stage love), Hastings and Constance come closest to being the conventional lovers of sentimental comedy but Goldsmith makes real people of them, thus giving extra weight to their rebellion. Gregory Floy's Hastings in the NT production was someone

uneasily aware of his awkward subordinate role and the equivoca-
tions and uncertainties surrounding his love affair, not least those
occasioned by Constance's determination to have her jewels as
well as her lover. There were interesting breaks in the assured,
dashing surface he normally presented, as in the scene when Tony,
incredulous at anyone offering to take over Constance, paints an
unflattering portrait of her: 'there's not a more bitter cantankerous
toad in all Christendom.' Hasting's wry aside, 'Pretty encouragement this for a lover', was a moment of real nervousness, though
he was soon offering, with his usual aplomb, to 'take this bitter
bargain off your hands'.

Constance, similarly, though hers is the standard situation of
sentimental comedy, is too much of an individual to be a standard
sentimental heroine. When she tells Hastings in Act V.ii that she
cannot go on with the elopement, she uses words like 'repentance',
stock currency of sentimental drama. But she has money, not
morality, in mind: 'In the moment of passion, fortune may be
despised but it ever produces a lasting repentance.' She is a cool-
headed, worldly and witty individual, who adds considerably to
the comedy with her lively talk and powers of improvisation, as in
the scene when she invents for Mrs Hardcastle's benefit a letter 'all
about cocks, and fighting', pretending it comes from Dick Ginger,
a name dragged out of Tony as the only person he can think of as
likely to write to him. There is pathos in this, as in the discovery,
humiliating for him as well as theatrically comic, that he cannot
read but must hand the incriminating letter to his mother for
further elucidation. It is characteristic that Constance has no sense
of the pathos; she is naturally enough engrossed with her own
drama, but the contempt she heaps on Tony in the recriminations
that follow is rather brutal. Yet she too suffers. She gets some fun
out of the pretence of flirting with Tony but she can hardly enjoy it
when his irritation results in his flinging her about. And she really
dreads her banishment to Aunt Pedigree's. 'If you knew what a
scene of constraint and ill-nature lies before me', she says to
Marlow, still resenting his betrayal by his friend, 'I'm sure it would
convert your resentment into pity.' Goldsmith makes her an interesting individual, not entirely sympathetic but with a charm
Tony is prepared to admit when he knows she doesn't really want
him. She draws out his lyrical gift, for he has observed 'her hazel

eyes, and her pretty long fingers, that she twists this way and that, over the haspicholls like a parcel of bobbins'.

Constance and Hastings hardly count as true rebels against the system. They get their own way in the end as a result of the benign atmosphere engendered by the agreement between Kate and Marlow – and Tony's eagerness to free himself of marriage obligations to Constance once he knows he is legally of age. 'Witness all men by these presents', he shouts delightedly, as he formally casts her off: 'So Constance Neville may marry whom she pleases, and Tony Lumpkin is his own man again'. But the scene in which the liberation occurs (V.iii) opened with the rueful return of the pair, and their public confessions of error; Constance blaming herself for succumbing to romance and 'in an hour of levity' being prepared 'even to give up my fortune to secure my choice'. This is a somewhat flawed happy ending.

Kate Hardcastle's is a fuller triumph. She makes the two figures of ultimate authority – her father and Marlow's – witnesses to her victory over the constraints placed upon her freedom to marry only someone she really knows and wants. She demonstrates that she knows Marlow better than either of the fathers, laying out the proof of it like a director organising a stage scene. Placed by her behind the screen (that most resonant stage property), they see Marlow on his knees declaring passionate love for her, though they had heard him swear he had only one interview with her and that 'formal, modest, and uninteresting'. 'This fellow's formal modest impudence is beyond bearing'; had not Mr Hardcastle seen with his own eyes Marlow embracing his daughter? A wave of chaos threatens to engulf them. But when Sir Charles brings the scene to an end, unable to stand his son's seeming hypocrisy, and Marlow discovers that the 'poor relation' is Miss Hardcastle, reason is restored on the instant. The scene is bathed in a good humour distinctive of Goldsmith, as in Mr Hardcastle's diplomatic summing up, 'I see it was all a mistake'. It is Marlow's final humiliation, to bare his reserved heart before an audience he does not suspect and would never have tolerated. But we are surely persuaded that this is a small price for all he gains. Kate is the goddess of the scene. It seems apt that her father should cast the wish for a happy ending in the form of a supplication to her on behalf of Marlow: 'I know she'll forgive you. Won't you forgive him, Kate?' and that she should be seen retreating with her lover to the 'Back Scene', still 'tormenting him'.

Tony Lumpkin's is the most tumultuous – and radical – of the three revolts by the younger generation: all the others, as we have seen, depend in some way on his mischievous energy. Goldsmith's clever blending of artifice and naturalness is at its most subtle with this character. For such an archetypal figure of farce, he is conceived in remarkably rounded terms. His colourful, homespun language and vigorous common sense often make him seem the most lifelike (and sane) person in the play. He hits the common note; as in telling his mother not to keep 'dinging and dinging it into one so', or when struggling to read Hastings' note: 'Then there's an "M" and a "T" and an "S", but whether the next be an "izzard" or an "R", confound me, I cannot tell.'

His sense of humour is easily tickled and he is uninhibited about showing it, which enrages Constance and Hastings, when their clever plots begin to go awry. Like Shakespeare's Puck, he finds the lovers' antics deliciously nonsensical. 'Here's another', he says, as an indignant Marlow approaches in Act IV.i, 'we shall have old Bedlam broke loose presently.' Yet he is sensitive to their criticism of him. When Constance calls him a 'stupid fool' for handing the incriminating letter to his mother, he fights back: 'By the laws, Miss, it was your own cleverness, and not my stupidity, that did your business.' But he is perturbed, all the same, as Goldsmith indicates by sending him into a *'reverie'* (the word in the stage direction) during the chorus of recriminations which ends in Constance being summoned to join Mrs Hardcastle in the carriage for the dire journey to Aunt Pedigree's. Marlow administers a last, grave rebuke: 'You see now, young gentleman, the effects of your folly.' And Tony emerges from his reverie with his latest ploy fully hatched. Like a comic – and humane – Iago, he exults in his own cleverness: 'Ecod, I have hit it. It's here.' The fantastic journey 'round and round' the house is there in his mind, down to the exact time it will take: Hastings is commanded to meet him at the bottom of the garden in two hours and Tony turns up, in Act V, in two and a half.

This is benign expiation: more than any of the others, Tony is willing to use his inventive powers altruistically, his only reward to be accepted, so he tells them, as 'a more good-natured fellow than you thought for'. But below the humane impulses lie more powerful drives. He enjoys himself in a manic way, it is clear from his account to Hastings, by putting the fear of God into his mother on the comic nightmarish journey: 'By jingo, there's not a pond or slough within five miles of the place but they can tell the taste of.' Some of Goldsmith's first hearers were worried by the threat of danger in this odyssey.[3] He reassured them by having Hastings ask, 'But no accident, I hope', and Tony reply that no one is really hurt; only 'mother is confoundedly frightened'. When Mrs Hardcastle appears, a pitiable figure, 'draggled up to the waist like a mermaid', in Tony's graphic phrase, he might enlighten her that she is in her own garden, but does not. Her worst time is still to come, as he wickedly evokes Crack-skull Common and invites her to suspect highwaymen behind the familiar trees. A mischievous Puck in eighteenth-century riding clothes, Tony is not fazed when Mr Hardcastle strolls on, taking his evening walk, but gets Mrs Hardcastle behind a tree and makes adroit use of warning coughs and easily misread phrases to keep her on tenterhooks.

The farce reaches its apogee when the terrorised Mrs Hardcastle, unable to hold back any longer, throws herself at her husband's feet and begs 'Take compassion on us, good Mr Highwayman'. Yet still, even in the midst of the hilarity some delicate human notes are struck, which should not be overlooked in performance. Goldsmith's genius consists partly in his ability to remind us in the midst of absurdity that not everything is absurd, it may be genuinely poignant, or tender. It is not just absurd, for example, when Mrs Hardcastle appeals to the 'highwayman': 'Take my money, my life, but spare that young gentleman.' Her role, like Tony's, calls for a comedian's arts, but the actress must be able to convince us, at such moments, that under all the fussing and falsity, there is a genuine love for her 'dear, sweet, pretty, provoking, undutiful boy'. We should not miss, either, the fatherly, even affectionate, tone of Mr Hardcastle's rebuke to Tony for driving the horses so fast: 'Forty miles in three hours; sure, that's too much, my youngster.' And Tony, his manic outburst spent, makes a fair point when he tells his mother with a kind of wry gravity: 'Ecod, mother, all the parish says you have spoiled me, and so you may take the fruits on't.' Mr Hardcastle is at last able to agree with him: 'There's morality, however, in his reply.' On a more caustic note, Mrs Hardcastle too wins sympathy when she comments tartly on the pompous effusions of Hastings and Constance in the final scene: 'Pshaw, pshaw, this is all but the whining end of a modern novel.' As always, we need to be alert to the 'out of character' remarks which are actually a reminder of how complicated any character really is.

On the symbolic level which Goldsmith establishes with such satisfying naturalness, Tony Lumpkin sweeps through the play in a gust of dionysiac glee, the spirit of subversion and free self-expression. He brings in the sound of music, letting himself go in bursts of hearty song that express his bucolic, anti-sentimental view of life. 'Rang do didlo dee', he trolls, as his mother cries at the failure of her attempt to make him woo Constance: 'Let her cry. It's the comfort of her heart.' A rustic Dionysus in the Three Pigeons scene, he delights the company with a song of his own making which dismisses everything he finds oppressive, from classical learning ('their Lethes, their Styxes, and Stygians') to Methodist preachers who denounce drink but always preach best 'with a skinful'. Goldsmith finally got his own back on the genteel audience who refused to accept his low bailiffs. Squeamishness is certainly given its *coup de grâce*, when the 'fellows' at the inn praise Tony's singing, 'bekeays he never gives us nothing that's *low*'/ 'Oh, damn anything that's *low*, I cannot bear it'. Low life claims its place in the entire scheme of things, in the person of Tony Lumpkin.

Despite the preposterousness of its initiating situation, *She Stoops to Conquer* convinces us that everything happens as it has to, given the nature of the characters and their drive to be themselves. Goldsmith had at last achieved in his writing for the theatre the quality of 'fable' which had charmed readers of *The Vicar of Wakefield* and *The Deserted Village*. Inspired by memory (the Irish memory that was so potent) he had finally been able to shape, from the depths of his experience, an artful, theatrical and yet wonderfully natural image of life's comedy.

6
Sheridan's Comedy of Masks: Harlequins and Thespians

The *commedia dell'arte* and its offspring, English pantomime, stretch a long finger into Sheridan's comedy. Disguisings, cheatings and ingenious improvisations are the order of the day in all his plays from *The Rivals* to *The Duenna*, while in *The Critic* the theatre scene simply swallows up a private world already obsessed with histrionics and turns everything to burlesque. *St Patrick's Day* and *The Duenna* are thick with disguises. Lieutenant O'Connor dresses up twice to deceive Lauretta's father, first as a 'country looking fellow', then as a doctor, while in *The Duenna* half the characters are in disguise half the time. The duenna disguises herself as her mistress, Louisa, who disguises herself as a nun, drawing from her lover, who fails to recognise her, the splendid line, 'Be quiet, good nun, don't tease me'. This is in the vein of a *Marriage of Figaro* or a *Cosi Fan Tutte*. Some characters maintain false identities without benefit of disguise, supremely Jack Absolute, who anticipates Wilde's Jack Worthing ('Jack in town and Ernest in the country') in his adroit juggling with his invented other self. He responds with the amused sangfroid of a Wildean dandy to Bob Acres' plea to deliver his challenge to the elusive Beverley. 'Well, give it to me and trust me he gets it', he says, and 'No trouble in the world, I assure you'.

The popularity of pantomime with Drury Lane audiences gets a sidelong look in *The Critic* when Mr Dangle reminds his wife, impatient with his theatre mania, that his contacts give her some advantages, including 'reading of the new pantomime a fortnight previous to its performance'. Pantomime provided a fashionable prototype for Sheridan's dashing adventurers in the Harlequin,

quintessential cheater and improviser. Behind him – and other
stock types of pantomime like Clown and Columbine – the line
went back through Marivaux, Shakespeare and Italian *commedia*
to the 'masks' of the classical theatre. Sheridan professed to know
few plays when he wrote *The Rivals*, but he was one of those, like
Goldsmith, who picked up hints and impressions with lightning
ease. The fact that he was writing in a high, ancient tradition of
comedy was certainly clear to him and must have added to the
exuberant confidence he shared, as a playwright, with his stage
personae. They display their knowledge of Shakespeare and other
writers with careless ease, in a profusion of quotation; casual,
correct, half-finished, garbled or run together, as the dramatic
situation requires. They place themselves neatly in the theatrical
tradition, as when Doctor Rosy interrupts his plotting on behalf of
the amorous lieutenant to brood like a conflation of Macbeth and
melancholy Jacques: 'Life's a shadow! – The world's a stage! – we
strut our hour.'

His enjoyment in playing variations on classic themes comes
through Sheridan's comedy with gusto, adding to the pleasure it
gives and joining itself in that way to Shakespeare's. In *Twelfth
Night*, one of the models for *The Rivals*, Shakespeare had adapted
a classical situation – the duel between reluctant combatants – to a
plot based on a girl disguised as a boy. With equal ingenuity
Sheridan adapts the 'impossible duel' to his own preoccupation
with split personality, giving his challenger a rival who exists only
as an aspect of another character. Sheridan's closeness to the
pantomime tradition (and perhaps his Irishness) often pushes him
to broad, manic effects on the edge of the utterly grotesque, as
with the proliferation of veils in *The Duenna* or O'Connor's wildly
extravagant impersonations. His jocose choice of surname for his
'countryman' role – 'Hum', meaning 'hoax' – nearly gives the
game away, even to the gullible Credulous. The masquerade becomes increasingly bizarre when he plays the doctor, diagnosing
Credulous' supposedly fatal condition in absurd gibberish: 'Palio-
vivem-mortem-soonem' (translated by the genuine doctor, Rosy,
as 'you have not six hours to live'). This is all in the style of
commedia scenarios like that of the seventeenth-century Harlequin who advises the Captain to cure his toothache by putting a
piece of apple in his mouth and holding his head in the oven till the
apple is baked: 'I'll answer for it if that won't cure your toothache.'

We might almost expect the eighteenth-century English Harlequin, Baxter, to bound on to Sheridan's stage at some point in *St Patrick's Day*, to join his disreputable confrères in mischief.

Comic opera also fuelled Sheridan's energetic variations on old themes. His sensitivity to musical phrasing and the support he received from the musical Linleys (their young friend, Nancy Storace, created the role of Susanna in *The Marriage of Figaro* in 1786) gave the genre an obvious attraction for him. But also it gave scope for some playful undermining of figures of authority, like parents and priests. His Whiggish, republican spirit found an outlet in such scenes as the guying of the drunken, lecherous friars of *The Duenna* or the unsparing caricature of Isaac Mendoza as a naturally avaricious Jew (an attitude rather hard for modern audiences to accept as pure fun). Sheridan had a precedent for his tuneful but often rough satire in *The Beggar's Opera* (1728) which had revolutionised music theatre with its politically charged portrayal of the ruling class in terms of a confidently singing, laughing and cheating underclass of highwaymen, prostitutes and informers. The Sheridan who was later to speak in the House of Commons on behalf of the French Revolution could not but have been drawn to this subversive genre. The key situation of *The Duenna* – Margaret's outwitting of her master – though its revolutionary overtones are more muted, does partly anticipate the witty victory of Mozart's servants over the Count in the most revolutionary of all comic operas, *The Marriage of Figaro*. Sheridan's Margaret has a more dubious triumph – winning Isaac Mendoza as a husband might be counted a disaster – but she starts from a lower base, being not only a servant and poor, but plain, unlike Mozart's delectable Susanna. Sheridan is not altogether kind to Margaret: he allows Isaac coarse jokes on her looks, as when he comments that 'the razor wou'd'nt be amiss for either of us'. His snarling account of her teeth to her own father is another uncomfortable sort of joke: 'where there is one of ivory, its neighbour is pure ebony, black and white alternately, just like the keys of an harpsichord.' But she gets the upper hand of him in the battle of insults which follows his discovery of how he has been tricked into taking her for Louisa. She wins a 'Well done, Margaret' even from Don Jerome with her riposte to Isaac's taunts about her plainness: 'Dares such a thing as you pretend to talk of beauty – a walking rouleau – a body that seems to owe all its consequence to the dropsy – a pair of eyes like two dead beetles in a wad of brown dough.'

Another opera of Mozart's, *Don Giovanni*, comes into view when Lopez, like Leporello prowling the streets of Seville with his dark lantern, deplores the anti-social hours his master's serenades make him keep: 'well, of all services, to serve a young lover is the hardest.' Philandering is not exactly Sheridan's theme – Ferdinand and Antonio are single-mindedly devoted to their respective girls – but a strong illusion of philandering is created by the disguises, and the jealousy roused among the confused young lovers is crucial to the plot, as in *Don Giovanni*. In the non-musical plays Sheridan continues to observe the convention of sharp, masterful servants which was so attractive to writers of comic opera. Lucy in *The Rivals*, delivering fake *billets doux* and taking bribes for assignations, can afford to disdain the abusive 'simpleton' hurled at her by an irritated Mrs Malaprop. Totting up her takings, she enjoys the joke of being typed as simple: 'Let me see to what account I have turned my *simplicity* lately.'

A standard scenario of both *commedia* and comic opera, conflict between an old and young man over the young man's right to marry where he pleases, is also Sheridan's favourite. He plays many variations on the heavy father, the 'senex' of *commedia*. There is testy Sir Anthony Absolute, nervous Justice Credulous and, in *The Duenna*, not one but two tyrannical fathers, each complacently sure that he has kept his daughter out of the arms of an unsuitable lover, each cheated into accepting the daughter's choice rather than his own. Characters such as these operate, up to a point, as fixed masks. Often they are summed up in a line or so, like the 'humours' of Ben Jonson, before they appear on stage, as in Fag's 'Absolute in everything or it would not be Sir Anthony Absolute'. Lydia's romanticism is fixed on her like a mask in her opening conversation with Lucy by her eager questions about the availability of romantic novels in the circulating library: 'And could you not get *The Reward of Constancy*? . . . Nor *The Fatal Connection*? . . . Nor *The Mistakes of the Heart*?' A moment or two later Mrs Malaprop also places herself in the terms laid down by her name, scolding Lydia for preferring a penniless ensign to Captain Absolute and demanding a promise 'to forget this fellow – to illiterate him, I say, quite from your memory'. In *The Duenna* another form of 'typing' comes with the music which, as in *The*

Marriage of Figaro, gives some of the best tunes to the social rebels. The running commentaries on all the performers (on and off stage) in *The Critic* show Sheridan's method at full stretch. Sir Fretful Plagiary, who makes only one brief appearance, in the first half of the play, is elaborately analysed by Sneer before his entry:

> *Sneer*:   He is as envious as an old maid verging on the despera-
> tion of six and thirty: and then the insidious humility
> with which he seduces you to give a free opinion on any
> of his works, can be exceeded only by the petulant
> arrogance with which he is sure to reject your observa-
> tions.
> *Dangle*:   Very true, egad – though he's my friend.
>   (I,ii,184)

When Sir Fretful arrives, pat on cue, he is a cause for mirth twice over; for being so touchily vain, and for conforming so exactly to Sneer's diagnosis. Like a puppet on a string (or like Puff's actors, absurdly obeying the stage direction to *'faint alternately in each other's arms'*) he solicits opinions on his new play and rejects them with just the 'petulant arrogance' that has been defined as his fixed mode. Mrs Dangle, who begins by discreetly finding no fault at all in the play ('Upon my soul the women are the best judges after all!') risks his wrath by wondering if it might be 'on the whole, a little too long'. Does she mean that it was 'tediously spun out'? When she hastily reassures him – 'O Lud! no, I speak only with reference to the usual length of acting plays' – he is pleased to put her right:

> Then I am very happy – very happy indeed, – because the
> play is a short play, a remarkably short play: – I should not
> venture to differ with a lady on a point of taste; but, on these
> occasions, the watch, you know, is the critic.
>   (I,ii,311)

He is completely restored to complacency by Mrs Dangle's con-ciliatory suggestion that 'it must have been Mr Dangle's drawling manner of reading it to me'. That would explain it, he agrees, and if she ever has three and a half hours to spare, he will read it to her himself, guaranteeing to show that it can be done in the time, even allowing 'for the music between the acts'. 'I hope to see it on the stage next', she neatly parries. Sheridan enjoys a double joke here: the audience will not be able to evade the experience Puff has in store, a play doubtless even worse than Sir Fretful's. But Sneer and Dangle will be on stage for the dress rehearsal, along with the besotted author, to filter *The Spanish Armada* through ironic commentary, part of the process that turns dullness to delight.

Satirical commentary on the absurdity of those who cannot see anything absurd about themselves is the root of all Sheridan's comedy. There is usually one character to represent sense and provide telling comments on the extravagant self-expression of the rest. *The Duenna* differs, in that there is no sustained ironic perspective from a character such as Sneer or Absolute. The main characters are all too sunk in their respective infatuations to be consistently sceptical. The young lovers are almost as absurd as the tyrannical fathers in this respect. They are, however, allowed spasms of ironical amusement by a plot which is built upon ironies, above all, that inherent in the situation of the cheater cheated. Antonio and Louisa enjoy an ecstasy of covert amusement when Isaac tells them (believing Louisa to be Clara) that he is going to carry off Louisa from her father's house by stealth and that 'tricking is all fair in love', a sentiment with which they heartily agree:

> *Isaac*: O lud, yes, ma'am – let anyone outwit me that can, I say – but here let me join your hands, there you lucky rogue, I wish you happily married from the bottom of my soul.
>
> *Louisa*: And I am sure, if you wish it, no one else shou'd prevent it.   (II.iv.83)

It is an artful three-cornered dialogue in which the audience hear the real meaning, closed to Isaac by his overweening sense of his own cleverness:

> *Isaac*: And what a laugh we shall have at Don Jerome's, when the truth comes out, hey?
>
> *Louisa*: Yes, I'll answer for't, we shall have a good laugh when the truth comes out, ha, ha, ha!   (II.iv.119)

The joke which is lost on Isaac is a form of punishment for self-satisfaction, as often with Sheridan's satire. Sneer's sardonic comments in *The Critic* serve a similar purpose. They are hardly needed to bring out the absurdity of the performance (which damns itself at every shriek and start), though they point it up amusingly. But they have an important function in demonstrating Puff's imperviousness to criticism and the gullibility of Dangle, quintessential theatre groupie. The entry of Burleigh, portentously mute, is a case in point. It is an opportunity for delicious silent comedy, as anyone knows who saw Ralph Richardson go through the motions required (enter, sit, get up, shake his head, exit) with stately complacency. The dumbshow gains an extra edge, however, from the busy commentary at the side of the stage. Puff cannot see anything funny about his anxiety for his friends to be silent, 'or you'll put him out'. When Sneer demands, 'Put him out! how the plague can that be, if he's not going to say anything?' his absurd reply is made in all seriousness: ' . . . why, his part is to *think*, and how the plague! do you imagine he can think if you keep talking?' 'He is very perfect indeed', Sneer's final comment, will clearly be wasted on the infatuated author – and add to the audience's enjoyment.

The presence of a sardonically sane commentator such as Sneer prevents *The Critic*, at least until its closing scenes, from being a totally obsessional farce. But Sneer is not a free-wheeling Harlequin. He is a fixed type, as his name indicates; 'born sneering', like Pooh Bah. His cynicism belongs partly with the other 'humours' which Sheridan likes to contrast with the mercurial Harlequin who can slide in and out of parts at will, misses no irony and revels in complications even when they turn against himself.

Jack Absolute is the epitome in this kind. 'Whimsical enough, faith!', he reflects, on discovering in Act III.i that 'my father wants to *force* me to marry the very girl I am plotting to run away with'. In true Harlequin fashion he immediately flings himself into his new role; dutiful son repenting his previous assertion that he would marry to please himself. He produces an unctuous rhetoric worthy of Joseph Surface, professing himself willing 'to sacrifice every inclination of my own to your satisfaction' and responding to his father's rapturous description of Lydia's charms ('lips smiling at their own discretion; and if not smiling, more sweetly pouting, more lovely in sullenness') with an amused 'thought' – 'That's she indeed?' – 'Well done, old gentleman!' – and a gravely impertinent spoken reply, 'And which is to be mine, Sir, the niece or the aunt?' Sir Anthony's rage over this insensibility blinds him to the unlikelihood of the 'reform'. 'I thought it was d–n'd sudden', he says when the truth about Beverley comes out, in Act IV. But he was taken in at the time by Jack's gleefully ironic performance of just the dull obedience previously demanded of him. It is a true Harlequin-style revenge which only the Harlequin himself can savour to the full. 'What's that to you, Sir?', Sir Anthony had asked, in Act II.i, when Jack had enquired, rather reasonably, the name of the bride intended for him. Completely in the grip of rage at Jack's display of independence, Sir Anthony became grotesquely irrational: 'the lady shall be as ugly as I choose: she shall have a hump on each shoulder; she shall be as crooked as the Crescent . . .'. Jack does not fail to remind him of this in Act III.i. He will marry, he says, to suit his father, not himself, though 'I own I should rather choose a wife of mine to have the usual number of limbs, and a limited quantity of back'. The corrective joke is missed by a father set, as always, on having his own way and stunned at his son's failure to appreciate his good fortune: 'What a phlegmatic sot it is! Why, sirrah, you're an anchorite! – a vile insensible stock.'

Everyone provides Jack with opportunities for ironic amuse-ment, including his own love, Lydia. Like his author (and perhaps most satirists) he is fond of the targets of his irony. He is good-humoured on the whole about his father's tetchiness, and though he does make fun of Bob Acres – the new clothes, the 'sen-timental' swearing – his teasing is affectionate. His is not a coldly detached amusement. He tries to make Faulkland see reason, intervening on one of his jealous fits with: 'Have done; how foolish this is!' It is only when reason proves unavailing that he stands back and enjoys the absurdity. Karl Johnson's Jack in the 1983 National Theatre production conveyed a half-pitying, half-mocking enjoyment of the build-up to inevitable explosion as Bob Acres in all innocence assured Faulkland that Julia had been well and happy in her lover's absence, driving him to distraction with talk of her spirited country dancing:

A Minuet I could have forgiven . . . had she made one in a cotillon – I believe I could have forgiven even that – but to be monkey-led for a night . . . to show paces like a managed filly! O Jack, there never can be but *one* man in the world, whom a truly modest and delicate woman ought to pair with in a country-dance; and even then, the rest of the couples should be her great uncles and aunts.

(II.i.247)

'Aye, to be sure!' Jack agrees ironically, 'grandfathers and grandmothers!' The irony is lost on Faulkland. Here, as often in the play, Jack is the only character on stage capable of relishing to the full the oddity of everybody else. Faulkland is too immersed in his fantasies ('the lascivious movement of the jig', the atmosphere 'electrical to love') even to notice Bob's eccentric expletives ('Odds swimmings' for Julia's graceful dancing) while Acres is completely out of his depth. 'The gentleman wa'n't angry at my praising his mistress, was he?', he asks Jack, as Faulkland storms out. Jack's dry 'A little jealous, I believe, Bob' is one of those many jokes he can share with no one – except, of course, the audience.

That Lydia is not exempt from his ironic scrutiny is made very clear earlier in this same scene when Faulkland expresses puzzlement about the impasse in his friend's love affair:

Faulkland: Why don't you persuade her to go off with you at once?

Absolute: What, and lose two thirds of her fortune? You forget that, my friend. No, no. I could have brought her to that long ago.

Faulkland: Nay then, you trifle too long – if you are sure of *her*, write to the aunt in your own character, and write to Sir Anthony for his consent.

Absolute: Softly, softly, for though I am convinced that my little Lydia would elope with me as Ensign Beverley, yet am I by no means certain that she would take me with the impediments of our friends' consent, a regular humdrum wedding, and the reversion of a good fortune on my side; no, no. I must prepare her gradually for the discovery, and make myself necessary to her, before I risk it . . .

(II.i.63)

Lydia is foremost among those Jack is tricking, as she bitterly recognises when the 'discovery' breaks, prematurely:

> So, while *I* fondly imagined we were deceiving my relations, and flatter'd myself that I should outwit and incense them all – behold! my hopes are to be crushed at once, by my aunt's consent and approbation! – and I am myself, the only dupe at last.
>
> (IV.ii.190)

She would scarcely have been mollified to hear the tall tale Jack invents on accidentally encountering his father in Act V.ii and needing to find a plausible reason for carrying a sword,[1] without revealing that he is en route for a duel. The story he improvises depends on Lydia being thought very silly. If she persists in refusing to forgive him for deceiving her, he tells his father, he intends to 'unsheath this sword – and swear – I'll fall upon its point and expire at her feet'. 'Fall upon a fiddle stick's end!' – Sir Anthony's disgusted grunt expresses a contempt for romanticism which seems not so different from his son's, to judge from Jack's summing up of his sweetheart's view of things: 'You know, sir, Lydia is romantic – dev'lish romantic, and very absurd of course.'

Warm-heartedness and cool, sceptical calculation of his own interests co-exist in this character. He does not scruple to deceive those close to him. Bob Acres is his dupe in the matter of the duel, and though this is a complication not of Jack's seeking – Acres insists on challenging his unseen rival, Beverley – it is Jack who keeps Beverley in existence and gets considerable amusement from his friend's nervousness:

> *Acres*:   If Beverley should ask you what kind of a man your friend Acres is, do tell him I am a devil of a fellow – will you, Jack?
>
> *Absolute*: To be sure I shall. I'll say you are a determined dog – hey, Bob!
>
> *Acres*:   Aye, do, do – and if that frightens him, egad, perhaps he mayn't come. So tell him I generally kill a man a week; will you, Jack?
>
> *Absolute*: I will, I will; I'll say you are called in the country 'Fighting Bob!'
>
> (IV.i.112)

he Critic has no tender moments of quite that kind: it is too
mitted to burlesque. But there is a humorous affection in the
ling of the theatre scenes which is part of a regular looking
o the real life of the audience. The first scene of Act II, set
re the curtain, gives the theatre staff of Sheridan's Drury Lane
hance to strike a note of solid reality. Mr Hopkins (chief
rer from Sheridan's dilatoriness in delivering his scripts) is
for by name; the under-prompter utters warnings about the
s' free cutting of the overlong text; Puff admits, 'I know I am
iant', Sheridan's joke against himself which he expects the
nce to share. We move outside the closed circle of farce in
expansive episodes while later we still keep in touch with
outside world through the sardonic viewpoint of Sneer. A
part of the pleasure in *The Critic* consists in seeing the
er elements at first contained, then getting steadily more
trollable. A deliberately cool framework is provided for the
ss to come. Mrs Dangle, at breakfast in Act I, has common-
enough, we might think, to keep any eccentricity in check.
aintains throughout her scenes the tart note struck in her
g question, 'Isn't it sufficient to make yourself ridiculous by
ssion for the theatre without continually teazing me to join
ven when the first wave of farce is let loose on her (in Act
her own drawing room – the linguistic babel of the Italian
and their French interpreter – she retains her rock-like
to be swept into chaos, announcing calmly to her husband:
ngle, here are two very civil gentlemen trying to make
ves understood, and I don't know which is the interpreter.'
as always, takes us a step nearer chaos by entering into
t; he beats out of time when the singing begins, and shows
hopeless inability to discriminate: 'Ah! Sneer! where will
such as these voices in England?' Sneer's languid 'Not
sures us that so long as he continues in the play, farce will
se its perspective totally. Even when the rehearsal gets
er way, with the thespians striking their ridiculous poses,
t always conscious of the sardonic figure at the side of the
minding us that there is a world of sense elsewhere.
, however, figures in *The Critic* only as a grand absurdity,
urina stark mad in white satin, her confidante the same in
n, and Whiskerandos reducing Puff's matchless rhetoric
se by ruthless cutting: ' . . . and must we part?/ Well, if –

The tone is light-hearted and can afford to be, Jack knowing that
Acres is perfectly safe from 'Beverley'. This duel will remain in the
world of jokes and teasing, unlike the really threatening one to
which Jack himself is later challenged by Sir Lucius and which he
accepts in a spirit of rage and resentment, caused by Lydia's
reaction to the Absolute/Beverley revelation. Sheridan allows his
nonchalant hero a moment of darker passion here, bringing him
closer to the violent Sir Lucius, as the latter jubilantly recognises.
'O, faith! I'm in the luck of it – I never could have found him in a
sweeter temper for my purpose' he says, overhearing Jack's ran-
corous 'thoughts' about his quarrel with Lydia: ''Sdeath, I never
was in a worse humour in my life! I could cut my own throat, or
any other person's, with the greatest pleasure in the world.'

The contrast between Jack and Faulkland as lovers is an ambiguous element in the play. Faulkland is an object of satire, Jack
an agent of it, so much is clear. But the sympathy is by no means
all one way. The man of sense may offer a necessary perspective
on the absurdities to which emotional sexual love is prone. But is
there something wanting in his sensible view, is there not something to be preferred in the romantic sensibility? Faulkland is
allowed to make the case for passion when, in Act II, Jack mocks
his woebegone look and exhorts him to 'love like a man'. His
moodiness, he protests, is a measure of his feeling:

Absolute: By heavens! I shall forswear your company. You are
the most teasing, captious, incorrigible lover! Do
love like a man.
Faulkland: I own I am unfit for company.
Absolute: Am not *I* a lover; aye, and a romantic one too? Yet
do I carry everywhere with me such a confounded
farrago of doubts, fears, hopes, wishes, and all the
flimsy furniture of a country miss's brain?
Faulkland: Ah! Jack, your heart and soul are not, like mine, fixed
immutably on one only object. – You throw for a large
stake, but losing – you could stake, and throw again:
but I have set my sum of happiness on this cast, and
not to succeed were to be stripped of all.

(II.i.79)

The irony of that 'aye, and a romantic one too' brings home in a
somewhat chilling way Jack's emotional distance from his 'little

Lydia', as does his failure to challenge Faulkland's suggestions that he is not deeply committed ('You could stake and throw again').

Is he then, after all, a calculating Restoration suitor at heart, someone on whom the 'sentimental' movement has made no impact? Or is he more in love than Faulkland can see, or his own emphasis on Lydia's fortune would suggest? These questions, which confront any actor playing the part, are part of the larger ones about the nature of Sheridan's comedy. How seriously is it to be taken, is it more farce than comedy, how much of the fullness of life, including psychological interest, is there to be found in it? And – most curious of questions, in a comedy so firmly based on romantic love affairs – how much sympathy is there for romance – or to go a step further, for characters under any kind of emotional stress? Sexual love seems to excite more mirth than sympathy on the whole. The grotesque reelings and writhings of Tilburina and Don Ferolo Whiskerandos are presented as burlesque, like *The Critic* as a whole. But their absurdity can be seen as only an exaggeration – in terms suitable to burlesque – of the absurdities of the jealous lovers in *The Duenna* or of jealous Faulkland and extravagantly romantic Lydia. There are few scenes where lovers engage simply in loving exchanges. Usually they are plotting or enjoying the joke against those they are cheating, as Louisa and Antonio do when Lopez takes Louisa for Clara. The lovers, whispering and laughing in the next room, with Lopez benevolently looking on, are in an ecstasy of mischief, not of sexual delight. Even Lydia, who loves her handsome Ensign, rates the enjoyment of cheating her aunt high in her list of love's pleasures.

Sheridan could have asked Jack's question, 'Am not I a lover; aye, and a romantic one too?', with regard to his own life. The stage direction at the very start of *The Rivals*, '*Coachman crosses the stage*', has been taken as a merry, private reference to a prank of his courting days, when he disguised himself as a coachman in order to be with his forbidden love, Elizabeth. His sympathy with rebellious lovers is hardly in doubt. But people who take themselves very seriously almost invariably strike him as absurd: lovers easily slip into that category, so are always liable to be targets of his satire. There is something Irish here too, perhaps, in this keen sense of the ridiculous; a wariness of sentiment, partly because the writer knows it can exert too strong a pull on the emotional part of him. The rhetorical excesses of *Pizarro* show just how thoroughly

Sheridan could let go when he reined in his

The man who wrote *The Critic* did also wr however; its enormous success was due, a elemental and tender feelings it dealt in. Fe feeling, is an integral part of Sheridan's co to lose altogether the ordinary, multifaric even in the obsessional mode of farce. Far hand in *St Patrick's Day* and *The Critic*, insistent reference out to the more varieg life; glimpses of more complex feelings, cl he plunges into his harlequin-like, comi shows himself a thinking young officer men's complaints about the poor service the local inn-keepers. Though amused at are deflected, to drink St Patrick's healtl less vagabonds'), he seems genuinely treatment meted out to them from the p my conscience, 'tis very hard that these ly have bread from the soil they woul consistency here with his spirited refus lous' contempt for his profession (Dr rather see his daughter in a scarlet fe soldier').

He defends his job – and his Iris refusing Credulous' offer to accept terms offered: 'Forswear your count result is that the Justice is won round nor is 'the most impudent dog I agreeing that the young man is righ *The Rivals*, decent feeling on the pa shown to lie beneath a crust of irasci very different from the unremittin Even Dr Rosy's obsession with his terms only so far. We begin by laug the anatomical compliments ('I sh such an arm for a bandage – veins t but by the end these backward loo behalf of the young lovers, in a w for all: 'So, joy to you, my little wish you may make just such a v we must – we must – and in that case,/ The less is said the better.'

The Duenna scarcely aims at any strong impression of realism: it operates throughout at the distance from plausibility which the conventions of comic opera allow. Sheridan takes advantage of the high degree of stylisation in the form to indulge in some hearty caricaturing. Much of it – like the fun he has with Margaret's plainness or Isaac's Jewishness – also recalls the Harlequin pantomimes, with their ruthless burlesquing of anything old or disabled that stands in Harlequin's way. Yet the operatic convention works the other way too. Characters can win sympathy, not just by plotting on the right side, as Margaret does (helping her young mistress as well as herself to a husband) but by being assigned good songs. Margaret's is a star singing role: she draws the audience to her partly by a melodious voice singing tuneful numbers (making Isaac's derision of her hoarseness a joke that turns back on the speaker). Music also makes the young lovers more expressive. Through their songs a flow of romantic feeling infuses an action which in other ways tends to laugh at the extravagances of romance. Thus Sheridan hints at the possibility of some real emotional life behind the stereotypes.

It is in *The Rivals*, however, that he treads most delicately the precarious path over the abyss of the absurd, to invite sympathy and serious interest for his characters as well as delight in their comicality. Contemporary audiences had no difficulty in appreciating this mix, as their indignant reaction to the original Sir Lucius O'Trigger showed: they took that Jonsonian fire-eater only too seriously, as an affront to the Irish. Similarly, the tortured relationship of Julia and Faulkland attracted considered critical judgements. For one reviewer the treatment of the pair was 'sentimental' in the best sense: it might even be described as 'metaphysical', he surmised. Twentieth-century productions have seldom explored the psychological aspect; more often Faulkland's jealousy and swings of mood have been exploited for broad comic effect; a strategy which makes Julia's role, in any case a difficult one, almost impossible. A more subtle emphasis was introduced by Peter Wood, in his 1983 production in the Olivier Theatre (from which the illustrations that follow will be drawn). Fiona Shaw and David Rintoul built up a remarkably convincing intimacy between the uneasy lovers, without sacrificing any of the fun. I will return to their performance, but first I want to look at some of the other ways in which Sheridan mixes realism and the absurd – and which Wood's production so cleverly captured.

The opening scene at once strikes the distinctive note with its combination of bustling reality and efficient exposition of a highly artificial plot. A glance at this scene is enough to show how Sheridan must have enjoyed poking fun at Puff's laboured exposition in *The Critic*, where Sneer is driven to ask 'as he *knows* all this, why does Sir Walter go on telling him?' and is rebuked for lack of gratitude: 'the less inducement he has to tell all this, the more, I think, you ought to be oblig'd to him; for I am sure you'd know nothing of the matter without it.' As Coachman and Fag charged across the open space of the Olivier Theatre, to meet in front of a soaring background panorama of eighteenth-century Bath, they drew the audience immediately into closeness with the place and the people in it. It seemed almost incidental that they were also providing us with keys to the plot, including the crucial information that 'Captain Absolute and Beverley are one and the same person'. Fag obviously enjoyed giving Coachman this tasty bit of news: he had moved up a rung or two in becoming personal servant to the young master and liked his former fellow servant to see his sophisticated new status:

> *Fag*:   Excuse my glove, Thomas: I'm devilish glad to see you, my lad; why, my prince of charioteers, you look as hearty! – but who the deuce thought of seeing you in Bath!
>
> *Coachman*: Sure, Master, Madam Julia, Harry, Mrs Kate, and the postilion be all come!
>
> *Fag*:   Indeed!
>
> *Coachman*: Aye! Master thought another fit of the gout was coming to make him a visit: – so he'd a mind to gi't the slip, and whip we were all off at an hour's warning.
>
> *Fag*:   Aye, aye! hasty in everything, or it would not be Sir Anthony Absolute!
>
> (I.i.5)

Coachman's outsider position – his dialect, his naïve way of mixing up gentry and servants in his account of the family – gives Fag his chance to show off and he takes full advantage, showing himself no bad psychologist in the lightning character sketches he offers of the gentry: Sir Anthony, 'hasty in everything'; Mrs Malaprop, 'an old tough aunt'; Lydia, so rich 'she feeds her parrot with small pearls' but 'a lady of a very singular taste'. He also builds up the urbane ambience of Bath in the very act of running it down: 'but d–n the place, I'm tired of it; their regular hours stupefy me – not a fiddle nor a card after eleven!'

The servants have a vigorous life in the play. *Commedia* influences are inevitably strong in this quarter; it could be a scene from almost any Italian scenario or comic opera when Fag and Lucy meet in Act II.ii, each engaged on artful business for their employers, each confident of overreaching the other. A tune hummed on Fag's entry reinforces the impression. But a solider real life comes in with the difference in their personalities. Fag stays just this side of insolence in his relations with the gentry, sometimes going too far, as when he announces Sir Anthony, on a visit to his son, simply as 'a gentleman' and is buffeted for trying to chat about him with his master on equal terms ('our father is wrath to a degree'). Lucy, more skilfully, plays the 'simplicity' card, deceiving everybody with total success – and an occasional interesting spasm of self-justification, especially where Sir Lucius is concerned: 'I have a little scruple of conscience from this deceit.' In contrast with this blasé pair, Bob Acres' servant, David, is an honest rustic; again a stereotype, one might say, but developed to the point where he proves his right to be considered his master's friend as well as his servant. He works hard to dissuade him from the duel with 'Beverley', putting arguments which Bob resists all the more warmly for secretly subscribing to them. The NT actors drew a touchingly human relationship out of their comical interchanges. David responded with kindly teasing to Bob's peacocking in his absurdly overdone new 'fashion' clothes ('Dress *does* make a difference, David') and was genuinely anxious about the duel, for which his master was so obviously unfit. Clown, in eighteenth-century pantomime, was often 'a gentleman's servant'. Sheridan gives his Clowns some solid human rights and keeps them a real presence in the play right to the end. It is David (accompanied by Fag, also worried) who warns Sir Anthony and the rest in the nick of time, so preventing the real duel between Absolute and Sir Lucius that has been running alongside the fantasy one as threatening obbligato. The anxiety of the two, on their humble, 'real life' level, invests the event with some gravity, an effect Sheridan clearly wanted.

The duel is a supreme example of his skill in handling well-worn theatrical material, not just to give it new comic sparkle but to invest it with a layer of more serious personal feeling and moral complexity. Wood's production brought out a sense of mounting tension and real fear (on the part of Julia as well as David and Fag) as the characters made their way to the duel venue at King's-Mead-Fields. Bob Acres' fear soon dissolves. Once he hears the truth about Beverley, he has no difficulty in refusing his friend's saturnine offer to fight with him on behalf of the absent one. He can put up with being called 'coward' by Sir Lucius: his relief fills the scene. Jack's willingness to fight with Sir Lucius, on the other hand, maintains just the exaggerated idea of 'honour' which Bob Acres' cowardice (like Falstaff's) puts into shrewd perspective. He tells his father that he accepted the challenge, because 'you know, Sir, I serve his Majesty'. The audience's sympathies are questioned at this point. Jack's careless courage is attractive, but Sir Anthony probably hits the mark for most of us when he barks: 'Here's a pretty fellow; I catch him going to cut a man's throat, and he tells me, he serves his Majesty!'

Sheridan's own ambivalent attitude to duels provides interesting colour shades in this episode. His dangerous fight with Mathews, still recent when he wrote *The Rivals*, provided a stimulus – possibly a compulsion – to write about a duel, and the seriousness of the wounds he had received, his closeness to death, must have helped to give force to the objections made to duelling in his play. The objections would be well to the fore in the audience's mind too, given the bad publicity duelling had received in the theatre, especially in the new sentimental plays. Goldsmith too had contributed a grim picture of the effects of duelling in *The Vicar of Wakefield*. Sheridan could not but have had all this in mind. Yet of course he also knew how he himself had ignored such objections in the Mathews affair. He put more of the murderous situation he had faced then into his first version of the play. Sir Lucius was much closer to the 'bloodthirsty Philistine' David describes in the revised one. 'Put him to death', he exhorted Bob Acres when spurring him on to challenge his rival. When obliged to soften the character, Sheridan made the fun more innocent but did not altogether lose the sense of something dark and sinister behind the amusing façade. The note was struck early in the duelling plot for the audience to the NT production. They were invited to feel some concern when Barrie Rutter's appealingly natural Bob Acres faced the pressure to fight from Philip Donaghy's also appealing but steely Sir Lucius:

Acres: But he has given me no provocation.

Sir Lucius: Now, I think he has given you the greatest provocation in the world. – Can a man commit a more heinous offence against another than to fall in love with the same woman? Oh, by my soul, it is the most unpardonable breach of friendship!

Acres: Breach of *friendship*! Aye, aye; but I have no acquaintance with this man. I never saw him in my life.

Sir Lucius: That's no argument at all – he has the less right then to take such a liberty.

Acres: Gad that's true – I grow full of anger, Sir Lucius! – I fire apace! Odds hilts and blades! I find a man may have a deal of valour in him, and not know it! But couldn't I contrive to have a little right of my side?

Sir Lucius: What the devil signifies right when your honour is concerned. . . .

(III.iv.69)

It is absurd but not so much so that we can afford to dismiss it as a joke; we are reminded that the joke might turn out to be on us when Sir Lucius demands: 'Do you think Achilles, or my little Alexander the Great ever inquired where the right lay?'

The shifting argument is part of a changing pattern of responses that keeps interpretation flexible. Stereotypes are both used and undermined or dissolved. The NT production captured a suitable degree of unpredictability with ingenious touches such as casting Mrs Malaprop much younger and more attractive than is usual. Geraldine McEwan was able to convince us that this vivacious woman could easily fancy herself as Delia, being courted by Sir Lucius for her charms despite having no money of her own. The casting brought out a playful side of the character which allowed for a rather charming, almost real flirtation with Sir Anthony. It met with the audience's approval when he offered her a little

consolation at the end, after the humiliations attending her dis-
closure that she, not Lydia, is 'Delia'.

The handling of this episode brought out the artfulness of Sheridan's balancing act between fun and feeling. McEwan's expect-
ant, flirtatious approach – 'pardon my blushes' – made her absurd
but also vulnerable. She had to face a barrage of male derision: Sir
Lucius' contemptuous – 'You Delia – pho! pho! be easy', followed
by his offer to hand her over to Absolute or Bob Acres and Bob's
woundingly 'referential' refusal, 'Odds wrinkles! No!'. Perhaps it
was no more than Mrs Malaprop deserved but McEwan's stricken
look made it impossible to take her discomfiture quite so coolly,
especially as it meant conniving with the casual male assumption
that a woman of 'nearly fifty' should have finished with sexual
expectation. Geraldine McEwan's easy vivacity contradicted that
assumption throughout. Sheridan would surely have sympathised,
at some level of the mind, being himself notoriously susceptible to
ladies of a certain age. He probably wanted the audience to take
with some seriousness, despite malapropisms, her denunciation of
Sir Lucius as a 'barbarous Vandyke', when he rejects her with such
brutality. Sir Anthony is given a line which suggests this. 'Come,
Mrs Malaprop', he says, 'don't be cast down – you are in your
bloom yet.' No doubt in a hard-edged, more misogynistic production that too could be said in such a way as to raise a laugh against
her. Michael Hordern's Sir Anthony, however, while enjoying the
joke, conveyed a genuinely kindly courtesy, as was only right,
given the pleasant little tête-à-têtes he had enjoyed with his partner in authority throughout the play, in their efforts to achieve
exactly what has been achieved: the marriage between Jack and
Lydia.

Wood's attention to the finer points of feeling brought out many
such revelations about character and opened up dimensions not
often explored in performance. Even the most eccentric 'humours'
characters were seen to have another side to them, sometimes to
be aware of their own fixedness. Hordern built up a rounded
human being in this way, as when he reflected drily, with just a
hint of humorous self-understanding, on Jack's refusal to marry to
order: 'An obstinate, passionate, self-willed boy! Who can he take
after?'

The malapropisms are a feature of the play which have usually
been taken just for fun. Of course they are very funny: Sheridan

had no need to fear comparisons with Mrs Malaprop's many predecessors in the mispronouncing line (his mother's novelistic creation included). His is the character whose name has entered the language as a generic term for the 'nice derangement of epitaphs'. The comedy of it was buoyantly upheld by Wood's company. But an extra layer of interest was added to the malapropisms by a more humane approach (characteristic of the production) which suggested at times a spirited, if chaotic, struggle for self-enlargement. McEwan conveyed an impression of someone with more energy than she could find outlet for; someone who longed to inhabit – and partly did – a more interesting world of the mind than that conventionally assigned to a middle-aged woman of her class and time. Curiously, she brought to mind another scatter-brained misquoter, from a very different realm, Beckett's Winnie. Like her, McEwan's Malaprop fished about in her memory for expressive words, sayings, proverbs, lines from Shakespeare. Her failures, like her garbled quotation from *Hamlet* – 'something about kissing – on a hill' – were comical, as they have to be, but, again like Winnie's, indicated something aspiring in the character which the audience could not afford to despise. How many of them, after all, could fill in correctly for her at every point? Not everyone will instantaneously supply the right word when she chides Sir Anthony for being 'an absolute misanthropy' or includes in her elaborately confused map of learning a wish that every young girl should have knowledge of 'contagious countries' or be 'a mistress of orthodoxy'. Gaps in the audience's laughter usually show where the erudite joke has gone beyond them and they are obliged to share in her all-too-human tendency to error.

Wood's sensitive production allowed for occasional glimpses into a psychological subtext by way of the absurd. It was the wrong word Mrs Malaprop used at her first meeting with Captain Absolute, when she complimented him on the 'ingenuity of his appearance'. Yet it was in a way the right one, as if a flash from the Freudian unconscious were warning her about the ingenious deceiver. McEwan's sharp, bright looks warned us not to think her too much of a fool: the character has her intuitions (and is by no means the only one deceived by Absolute). That other wrong word, 'orthodoxy' also had a kind of surreal plausibility with its covert reference to her own unorthodoxy, in sexual as well as linguistic matters. Perhaps some nervousness over the 'Delia' episode and how reprehensible people might think it supplies her with the particularly absurd mistake which closes her educational advice: a girl should learn to spell and pronounce correctly 'that she might reprehend the true meaning of what she is saying'.

Softening touches such as those arrived at by McEwan and Hordern did not prevent Mrs Malaprop from being the 'tough old aunt' required by the plot. The clash between heiress and guardian is necessarily conventional, up to a point, but it gained fresh new colour in Wood's production from Mrs Malaprop's relative youthfulness, which introduced a frisson of sexual jealousy into the relationship of niece and aunt. Lydia identifies this in Act I.ii, making a connection between her aunt's harsh behaviour following her discovery of the 'Beverley' romance and her infatuation with 'a tall Irish baronet'. 'Then, surely, she is now more indulgent to her niece', Julia says, innocently. Seventeen-year-old Lydia knows better: 'Since she has discovered her own frailty, she is become more suspicious of mine.' It is a battle of wills she intends to win. The soulful Miss Languish is shown to have scant sympathy with her aunt's romantic cravings, dismissing contemptuously her correspondence carried on 'under a feigned name . . . a *Delia* or a *Celia*'.

Anne Louise Lambert's purposeful Lydia was no little silly. Her passion for romance, which her lover considers so absurd, seemed only partially the 'caprice' everybody in the play takes it for. It was also a way of asserting her personality in face of intolerable pressure. Mrs Malaprop's refusal to allow her any say in her choice of a husband ('What business have you, Miss, with *preference* and *aversion*? They don't become a young woman') is comically expressed. But if Absolute and Beverley had not been one and the same person, Lydia's situation would have been no joke. Laughter comes to seem only dubiously the right response as the authoritarian pair hold forth about the best ways of keeping the young in order. Sir Anthony recalls how he dealt with objections from Jack as a boy by knocking him down and advises Mrs Malaprop to subdue Lydia by locking her up: 'and if you were just to let the servants forget to bring her dinner for three or four days, you can't conceive how she'd come about!' Lydia's appetite for romantic reading took on a new look in this context. Like that other determined heroine, Goldsmith's Kate, she is resolved to marry according to her own taste and romantic novels could be seen as a way of expressing – and feeding – her rebelliousness. Lydia is in fact a more modern kind of person than her name, 'Languish', or the titles of those sentimental novels would suggest. She is not sentimental in the modern sense of being 'soft'. Her affinity is with those super-sharp, conquering girls of *The Importance of Being Earnest*, constructing scenarios for their love adventures – to which the male is expected to conform. Cecily reads to Algernon (doubling as the mythical 'Ernest') extracts from the diary in which she recorded the details of her engagement to him, before they met. They include a ritualistic breaking off, necessary, she explains to the bemused Algernon, because 'it would hardly have been a serious engagement if it hadn't been broken off at least once'.

Lydia, similarly, intends her lover to fit in with her idea of how love should be. 'Beverley' has failed to live up to her scenario in one respect, as she explains to Julia (surely, as at the NT, with witty, Wildean playfulness). He was admirably romantic in most ways,

> 'But, I don't know how it was, as often as we had been together, we had never had a quarrel! And, somehow I was afraid he would never give me an opportunity. So, last Thursday, I wrote a letter to myself to inform myself that Beverley was at that time paying his addresses to another woman. I sign'd it *your Friend unknown*, shew'd it to Beverley, charged him with his falsehood, put myself in a violent passion, and vow'd I'd never see him more.
>
> (I.ii.76)

The elaborate fantasy would have been maintained for 'three days and a half', had not reality, in the person of Mrs Malaprop, intervened. Jack may take a patronising tone to Lydia's romanticism – but he has to toe the line. Wilde's Jack prepares to have himself christened, to satisfy Gwendolen's insistence on marrying an 'Ernest'. So, too, Sheridan's Jack, in his 'Beverley' persona, must assist in the acting out of Lydia's dream. It is a kind of feminist dream of sexual freedom. Lydia loathes above all the thought of being bought and sold like a 'Smithfield bargain'. Her caprices follow a marked pattern, a struggle to assert herself. Her outburst to Julia in Act V.i, when rope ladders and moonlight meetings have vanished, along with 'Beverley', includes a graphic sketch of the dominant role their romantic relationship allowed her. She relishes the memory of those uncomfortable assignations he endured for her on cold January nights, 'in the garden, stuck like a dripping statue'. This is not just romantic vapours; her glee has the ring of truth, as has her pettishness at the thought of the conventional marriage she knows she is doomed to, with its unpalatable accompaniments; the 'simpering' procession to the altar, the 'unmannerly fat clerk' calling the banns: 'Oh, that I should live to hear myself called spinster!' (only half a joke, as Anne Louise Lambert played it).

She is so far from being a sentimentalist as to jest rather sharply about Julia's troubled love affair. Gratitude for being saved from drowning played a part in it, we learn from the girls' first conversation (I.ii). This might have been expected to appeal to romantic Lydia, but not so. 'Why a water-spaniel would have done as much!' she laughs, 'Well, I should never think of giving my heart to a man because he could swim!' It is only a joke, she assures Julia, who takes it amiss. But the difference between the two girls lies here; it is another source of the psychological interest which conventionally comic performances tend to diminish or miss altogether.

Julia expresses her feelings more directly and openly, not under cover of pranks and jokes. She would 'chide' her friend, for being so silly, she tells her after the outburst in Act V.i, by laughing heartily at her; but she is not 'in spirits'. Hers is the most difficult part in the play, calling for a kind of endurance which risks seeming slavishly submissive: 'slave' is Lydia's word for it. The NT production achieved a rare seriousness in the presentation of Julia and her difficult lover. Fiona Shaw and David Rintoul made them interestingly real people, he tormented and neurotic; she, tormented but buoyantly sane and resilient. Shaw's Julia, tall, robust, quizzically humorous, was no patient Griselda, waiting for opportunities to suffer. She was putting up with Faulkland's tantrums because she needed to, being much in love. She did not hide her exasperation but tried, in a very natural, convincing way, to play down his faults as long as she could, making a case for him as someone ill at ease with social refinements; 'Unus'd to the fopperies of love', as she puts it. She assures Lydia in their first scene that 'he is too proud, too noble to be jealous', an assertion immediately contradicted (for the audience) in the following scene, when

Faulkland raves about Julia's ability to be happy in his absence.

How long will she put up with this absurd jealousy, we have to ask, and why should she? The actors supplied convincing reasons. Rintoul presented the character as an attractive but deeply insecure young man trapped in some obsession almost out of his control. His awareness of being trapped brought him sympathy – which in turn made Julia's position more tenable. He knew he was wrong to have so little faith, but seemed unable to drag himself out of doubt and suspicion. Rintoul gave poignancy to the self-scrutiny of Act III.ii when he wrestled with conflicting emotions: 'How mean does this captious, unsatisfied temper of mine appear to my cooler judgement! . . . I am conscious of it – yet I cannot correct myself.' Sheridan was interested in this neurosis as Goldsmith was in Marlow's. By allowing Julia understanding and tolerance, he gave her a similar role to Kate's, that of potential healer. Fiona Shaw's vigorous plain-spokenness kept the interest at a serious level; no specious mistakings and false impressions here. She had no doubt he was in some way ill, and would cure him if she could. His absurdity still drew laughs but they were tempered by a sense of the awfulness of his condition, for both of them:

Julia:	Must I never cease to tax my Faulkland with this teasing minute caprice? – Can the idle reports of a silly boor weigh in your breast against my tried affection?
Faulkland:	They have no weight with me, Julia: no, no – I am happy if you have been so – yet only say, that you did not sing with *mirth* – say that you *thought* of Faulkland in the dance.

(III.ii.36)

The audience laughed, but something rather infantile and desperate in his use of the third person allowed Shaw's Julia to respond on a serious note, reassuring him with almost maternal tenderness: 'I never can be happy in your absence.' Their dialogue swung to and fro, charting his neurosis with exactitude, from his gleams of reason – 'Oh, I am a brute when I but admit a doubt of your true constancy' – to agonised insecurity. She had only to use a word like 'gratitude' or mention the marriage contract with Faulkland to which her dead father had committed her, for his self-doubt to swell up. Shaw demonstrated that an intelligent performance could make Julia's potentially monotonous, 'virtuous' responses both interesting and natural. She managed to suggest that she was doing no more than any woman in love to make the best of a difficult lover, and reacting to his absurdities with a mixture of sad affection and irritation, as in her demand (Act III.ii), 'For what quality must I love you?'

Sheridan gives occasional glimpses into the dark pit of misogynistic fears over which Faulkland struggles to keep his balance. His remorseful soliloquy when Julia leaves the room in tears is one such. If he ever so distresses her again, he tells himself:

> may I lose her for ever! and be linked instead to some antique virago, whose gnawing passions, and long-hoarded spleen, shall make me curse my folly half the day, and all the night!

The bizarre, unpleasant sexual image was delivered by Rintoul partly as a joke (like the hard jokes against plain women in *The Duenna*) but with a touch of nervous revulsion which hinted at more deep-seated inhibitions. It became psychologically believable that his next action would be the elaborate 'test' he devises for Julia's faithfulness, the melodramatic tale of being obliged 'to fly this kingdom instantly' because of involvement in a duel (a perverse distortion of his harmless involvement in Jack's duel, as his second). It was equally believable that Julia should finally revolt when she realised that he had invented the story: he crassly expresses delight at having proved her 'to the quick'. He had gone too far, Fiona Shaw made us feel, because she had been induced to reveal her feelings with abandon, offering to accompany him to exile, even without his first marrying her; an incontrovertible proof of her faith in him. The force of her anger was in proportion to the force of her expression of love; and it was the shock therapy Faulkland needed. Convincingly, step by step, the actors brought us to the reconciliation which follows his contrition. The pious generalisations with which Julia ends the play were given fresh, personal interest by Shaw's intonation and sidelong glances which conveyed a warning to her lover: happy endings are fragile and will need to be continually defended from 'ill-judging passion'.

In the psychologically sensitive context established by the NT production, the Absolute/Beverley masquerade on which the whole plot turns came to seem much more than an amusing device to humour the romanticism of a seventeen-year-old. It was to do with the hero's character as well as the heroine's. In 'acting' Beverley, Karl Johnson's Jack seemed to be expressing something real in a personality more complex than might first appear. It is a curious harmony, after all, between the coolly rational, witty, plotting self and the romantic, emotional self he 'acts'. The occasional near-misses and final failure of his impersonations (they break down, significantly, when his father joins Lydia and Mrs Malaprop as his audience, in Act IV.ii) only drew attention to the difficulty of his assignment and his skill in persuading his audiences, even for part of the time, that he was what he claimed to be. Could the performance be so convincing if it did not draw on elements in the character's 'real' self? With this question we are in the Wildean territory which hovers on the edge of Sheridan's comedy, anticipating the existentialist plays about playing which have fascinated the modern theatre. Jack is likely to attract the interest of a modern audience, not just for his wit and charisma, but for the touches of darkness about him, including his masterful ability to deceive. Absolute/Beverley could be seen as a kind of innocent anticipation of Joseph Surface; innocent because he is affectionate (Joseph feels tenderness for no one).

The capacity for affection, somewhat equivocal, as we have seen, where Lydia is concerned, shows most strongly in his relationship with his father. Michael Hordern's predominantly jovial Sir Anthony may have slightly softened the rougher, authoritarian side of the character, but he realised another side which is equally clear in Sheridan's text, the deep wish for good relations with his son. It is reciprocated by Jack, who has remarkable tolerance for his father's tempers. An ironical comment, 'Mild, gentle, considerate father', is his reaction to the bullying episode of Act II.i which ends with Sir Anthony's storming out, threatening: 'I'll disown you, I'll disinherit you, I'll unget you! – And d–n me, if ever I call you Jack again!' When he found that Jack had only been acting indifference to Lydia's charms, Hordern's delighted reaction – 'I'm glad you have made a fool of your father, you dog – I am' – was a cry from the heart. The same warm feeling flowed in the final scene when Jack apologised to Sir Lucius for any unintended slight he had given him but declared his intention of defending his right to Lydia 'against any man whatever'. Sir Anthony clearly announced his love for his son in his shout of support: 'Well said, Jack, and I'll stand by you, my boy.'

His humane handling of personal relationships – among families, friends, lovers – is a major source of the affection audiences have felt for Sheridan's comedy. The human touches are no less recognisable for occurring in a context of supreme theatricality. This is indeed Sheridan's special triumph, to keep the histrionic and the humanly real in effective tandem. Julia, recognising that her patience with Faulkland is in danger of encouraging an 'incorrigible fault', that he is perhaps a man who can never be content or 'confident in love', is obviously a character to be taken seriously. But so is Jack; his harlequin pranks and high-spirited ways express a complex personality in comical near-surreal form.

At the start of his career Sheridan seems to have felt a pressure to be 'new'. In his preface to *The Rivals* he blames some of its original faults on his ignorance of 'plays in general, either in reading or at the theatre', laying a rather curious stress on this ignorance. It protected him, he said, from unwitting plagiary. He had been reading more than he was prepare to admit, however, for he proceeds to muse on the difficulties of distinguishing between invention and recollection: 'Faded ideas float in the fancy like half-forgotten dreams', and the imagination begins to doubt 'whether it has created or adopted'; an interesting glimpse into the artist's thought processes. It is obvious from the play itself that, like all eighteenth-century playwrights (and maybe those of any century), he was ready to 'steal with dignity', in Garrick's phrase. Far from trying to avoid echoes, he draws attention to the influences operating on him, as by way of jokes an audience brought up on Garrick's Shakespeare would instantly recognise; Bob Acres' garbled quotations from *Macbeth* and *King Lear*, for instance; 'The thunder of your words has soured the milk of human kindness in my breast! Zounds! as the man in the play says, "I could do such deeds!"' At every point the characters in the comedies are unmistakably linked to theatrical tradition. With Mrs Malaprop Sheridan even insisted on resurrecting a stereotype so familiar to his audience (Mistress Quickly and Dogberry had had many eighteenth-century successors) that there had been a call for a temporary abstention. Goldsmith's influence is clearly detectable too, in the importance to Sheridan of servants and low-class characters and in his handling of romantic love. Jack's strategy of 'stooping' in order to conquer Lydia has marks of Kate's device upon it, while the split personality ingeniously worked out in terms of farcical mistake in *She Stoops to Conquer*, has an equally ingenious successor in Jack's invention of Beverley.

Into this traditional material, with its familiar conventions, Sheridan poured a new psychic energy derived from his own life and personality. So ripe to his hand was the material he selected, so well did he adapt it to his imaginative needs, it could almost be said that the comic tradition was waiting for Sheridan to come along and provide its eighteenth-century gloss.

7
'The School for Scandal'

'Surface', the key name in the play, is the key to its interpretation. It is a comedy about the difficulty of getting at the truth of things, the ease with which people can be deluded by false surfaces. The whole of Act I and part of Act II are set among the scandal-mongers, who are seemingly engaged full-time in the business of falsification, blackening character and blowing up rumours and wisps of gossip into full-bodied, "circumstantial' accounts. The theme of 'false impressions', staple of sentimental comedy, is given a new twist which relates it to Sheridan's personal experience and to his psychological penetration, not least into himself.

When he returned to the National Theatre in 1990 to direct *The School for Scandal*, Peter Wood seized on this theme, projecting it through bold scenic as well as acting strategies. The programme struck the dominating note at the start: its front cover showed two fashionable people gossiping, cartoon style, balloons covered with eighteenth-century newsprint issuing from their mouths. On stage an emblematic chandelier in tree form sprouted newsprint tongues, the furniture wore newsprint covers and the play opened with a dumbshow (added by Wood) in which people ran around, delivering and reading scandal sheets. Lady Sneerwell was first disclosed to view reclining in a sumptuous four-poster bed, reading a magazine which obviously related to her principal interest in life: 'reducing others to the level of my own injured reputation.' Flicking tongues in the scenery, sibilant, snake-like hissing in the very sound of the names: there was no doubt from this staging where the core of the play was located.

The scandalmongers formed, in fact, a beau monde to which all the characters related in some way. It was an interpretation en-

couraged by the play's odd dramatic structure. By conventional
standards a disproportionate time is given to characters who are
minor in terms of plot; Snake, Mrs Candour, Lady Sneerwell
herself. They have the whole of a long first scene to themselves
and a still longer one in Act II. Wood's production made it clear
that these peripheral people were not so minor, after all. Rather,
they were a powerful magnet, drawing nearly all the main characters to them at one time or another, and having an insidious effect
even upon those who disapprove of malicious gossip, as Maria and
Sir Peter Teazle do. The latter is a reluctant visitor to Lady
Sneerwell's salon, as he tells the audience in an apprehensive aside
on his entry in Act II: 'Mercy on me, a character dead at every
word.' He is there only because of Lady Teazle's commitment to
the Sneerwell school. But that is itself a proof of scandal's power
to reach out into every kind of life. Scandal, it seems, is an
infection which only the strong can resist. The Surface brothers
separate themselves along this line. Joseph is at the heart of the
'school'; Charles is not seen anywhere near it. His absence is made
all the more striking by the fact that he is such a favourite topic
there. Everyone talks avidly about him, but he remains a distant
figure: it is not until halfway through the play, in Act III.iii (after
the interval in Wood's production) that this much discussed
character is seen in person.

Is this long delayed entry just loose plotting by Sheridan? As
usual, he had needed to cut a longer first draft; his many revisions
of the text might well have affected its proportions. However, all
we know of Sheridan's dramaturgic powers (his taut reworking of
The Relapse is a case in point) supports the view that the rather
curious structuring is deliberate. The long delayed entry of Charles
has one very important effect. It places the audience in the position of not knowing for themselves; they are persuaded to form
judgements on character from hearsay; a common situation of life
which Sheridan makes the thematic as well as dramatic pivot of the
play. Sir Peter has arrived at a prejudiced view of Charles by not
listening to the right counsel from Rowley, who insists on the
rake's good qualities and perhaps, despite his contempt for the
scandalmongers, by listening too much to the scandal they circu-
late. Sir Oliver, on the other hand, resists the pressure to typecast
Charles, either on Sir Peter's word or Rowley's, but goes to see for
himself – at which point and not before, the audience are given the

chance to make their own minds up about the character who arouses such disparate emotions. It is even then not an altogether easy process, as we will see. The curious structural arrangement which keeps Charles out of view for so long can therefore be taken as a paradigm of the difficulty universally experienced in getting to the real self of others.

Sheridan chose the word 'Scandal' for his title very consciously, rejecting his first thought, 'The Slanderers'. The intention may have been to soften the original concept, 'scandal' being a less black word than 'slander'. But it could equally be seen as a way of putting emphasis on the communal aspects of the theme. Scandal is, as the play shows, something that is spread by delighted consent: it can be also a kind of horrid art, one that can be learnt and taught. The scandalmongers come to Lady Sneerwell's as to a centre of excellence where they can practise and perform before an expert circle. Lady Sneerwell opens the play with a kind of tutorial, checking on Snake's completion of his assignments:

Lady Sneerwell:	The paragraphs, you say, Mr Snake, were all inserted?
Snake:	They were, Madam, and as I copied them myself in a feigned hand there can be no suspicion whence they came.
Lady Sneerwell:	Did you circulate the report of Lady Brittle's intrigue with Captain Boastall?
Snake:	That's in as fine a train as your ladyship could wish. In the common course of things I think it must reach Mrs Clackitt's ears within four and twenty hours – and then, you know, the business is as good as done.

Wood stressed this notion of a busy and pleasurable communal activity by another invented piece of dumbshow. A tapestry was brought in for the scandalmongers to work at, sitting on a long couch and stitching as they gossiped. It suggested that a kind of double art work was being shaped, in which young apprentices like Lady Teazle practised their skills along with such experts as Joseph Surface, Snake and Mrs Candour. All was pleasant, amusing – and deadly. What counted was effect, as Joseph Surface, played with youthful aplomb by Jeremy Northam, most cleverly realised. Like the modern upper-class con man, at home in a Mayfair restaurant, to whom Benedict Nightingale compared him,[1] he simply took it for granted that presentation was all. Lady Sneerwell's 'school', for him, was a microcosm of the world outside, indeed *was* that world. For the larger part of the play, after all, the valuations made in this 'glittering gossip shop' seem likely to decide his own and his brother's fortunes. Sir Peter continues until as late as Act V to believe that Joseph is a 'man of sentiment and acts up to the sentiment he professes' and that Charles has dissipated 'any grain of virtue' he might have inherited. These are images promulgated by the Sneerwell circle. Its emphasis on the power of plausible presentation makes *The School for Scandal* very much a play for our advertisement-oriented era. Wood's set lacked only a television screen to spell out the point.

The play acquired a layer of dynamism here which helped to counteract the softness threatened by the glossy visual charm and joviality of the production. Wood's glamorous looking world was at the other extreme from the more saturnine, decayed and vicious background Jonathan Miller created for the characters. Wood's indeed may have been the most sumptuous production of the play ever seen in the English theatre. No one else, not even Olivier in 1948, nor Gielgud (who directed what Peter Lewis called a 'velvet clad, fan wielding' production in the sixties)[2] had the same technical resources at his disposal. Elaborate mechanisms such as the Olivier Theatre's revolve-cum-lift may have tempted Wood into more visual peacocking than Sheridan intended. Sir Oliver made his first appearance not outside Sir Peter's house, as in the original, but disembarking from a grandly visible ship, followed by a train; Indian servant and baggage; the 'little nabob' in all his richness. But the glossiness had its own relevance to the image-making and self-advertisement which came over for most reviewers as a central preoccupation of the play. The modern note was at its sharpest in the presentation of Joseph's cool self-interest. For Jeremy Northam's blandly busy character, scandal was no pleasant frivolity, still less a bitter passion, as for Sneerwell, but merely useful; a form of discourse that needed only a few skilful pushes from a clever calculator to send it in a direction favourable to his ambition. This range of divergent motivations among the 'school' made the action exceptionally lifelike and plausible.

The almost universal complicity with scandal in the play hints to the audience that they may need to consider their own moral attitude to its delights. They are clearly not immune if they are laughing at Mrs Candour and the rest – and if they are not, the play has failed. But of course they always do. Thus the scandal scenes draw us into an ambiguous moral zone where laughter is at slightly uneasy variance with what we perhaps ought to feel about these essentially cold-hearted people. The NT audience sometimes voted by laughter against the morally edifying view. They might in serious mood have supported Maria's complaint – 'Wit loses its respect with me when I see it in company with malice' – but they laughed sympathetically with Lady Sneerwell when she flashed back: 'Pshaw, there's no possibility of being witty without a little ill nature. The malice of a good thing is the barb that makes it stick.'

Wood's humanising of the scandalmongers aided the process of self-identification which Sheridan clearly did not want his audience to escape. In the prologue Garrick wrote for the play, its author was presented as a youthful champion, a Don Quixote tackling a monster, 'this hydra Scandal in his den'. Wood's casting minimised the monster look. Jane Asher was an unusually youthful and seductive Lady Sneerwell, someone who could easily be imagined attracting the beau monde to her salon; the first glimpse of her in her lush bed, waited upon by Snake, struck an erotic note which was evidently part of the enjoyment her circle expected to experience in visiting her. On a more homely note, Prunella Scales' Mrs Candour, a cosy, friendly lady with grey curls, exuded the deadly niceness which Joseph diagnoses so accurately before her entrance: 'Whenever I hear the current running against the characters of my friends, I never think them in such danger as when Candour undertakes their defence.' Streaks of coldness punctuated the jollity as she dealt lethal wounds to reputation under cover of sympathetic concern. We might have thought her genuinely kindly when she followed Maria (who had left the room in agitation after hearing Charles maligned) to offer her assistance. But the 'kindness' ends in malicious innuendo: 'Poor dear girl, who knows what her situation may be!' Part droll and intimate (few of the innuendos failed to draw a laugh), part hard and unpleasant; the scandal scenes provoked sympathy and alienation in more or less equal measure, as they might in real life. Candour was repellent in professing a wish to comfort Lady Teazle as a reason for gaining admittance to her house in Act V, after the screen debacle. Her syrupy 'I am sure she must be in great distress' could by that stage in the play be taken as nothing but odious hypocrisy. Yet in the next breath she had the audience laughing with conspiratorial enjoyment as she confided her real motive for wanting to break past the servant who bars all visitors: 'Dear heart, how provoking! I'm not mistress of half the circumstances. We shall have the whole affair in the newspapers with the names of the parties at length before I have dropped the story at a dozen houses.'

An artful double perspective was maintained until the final collapse of Lady Sneerwell, at the end of the play. The characters were distanced by their caricature ways and names: Snake, Backbite, Crabtree. Yet for a modern audience, accustomed to television journalists gossiping nightly about the news and quoting sources frenetically, the scene in Act V.i when the 'school' swop rumours is almost a slice of life:

Sir Benjamin: I tell you, I had it from one –
Mrs Candour: And I have it from one –
Sir Benjamin: Who had it from one, who had it
Mrs Candour: From one immediately.

Sheridan plays a long cat and mouse game with the scandalmongers in Act V.ii, allowing them plenty of rope to hang themselves (and amuse the audience) with their false stories before administering a dose of truth. Crabtree won applause from the NT audience with his inventive 'circumstantial' account of the duel that never happened between Sir Peter and Joseph (or was it Charles, the gossips are not sure). It is a virtuoso piece of embroidery indeed, down to the last fine detail of the shooting; how Sir Peter was seriously injured, while his own bullet ricochetted from 'a little bronze Pliny that stood on the mantelpiece' and wounded the postman, just then coming to the door, 'with a double letter from Northamptonshire'. This is near-Pirandellian territory, except that the audience (in the auditorium) know what the facts really are and are waiting for the *coup de grâce* which comes when Sir Peter strolls on, to be greeted by Sir Oliver with an irony pointedly directed at the stage audience: 'Why man, what do you out of bed with a small sword through your body, and a bullet lodged in your thorax?'

This is general satire but the scandal motif is also used as a litmus test for individual psychology. It is a crucial factor in the Teazle marriage. Sheridan clearly places himself as a man of sentiment in handling that classical situation of the Restoration stage: old bachelor married to young girl fresh from the country. Just as clearly, he strikes the satiric Restoration note; it is his distinctive blend. For Wycherley in *The Country Wife*, Congreve in *The Old Bachelor* (a play Sheridan's characters refer to obliquely) satire was the only appropriate mode of approach to a marriage which so obviously asked for trouble. Sheridan allows scope to that view in his presentation of the quarrelling Teazles. For much of the play the pair are seen from the mocking perspective of the scandalmongers. When Mrs Candour tells Maria unpleasant rumours about the state of her guardian's marriage or Backbite promises Lady Teazle scurrilous stories about her own husband, we come very close to the Scandals and Tattles of the predecessors admired by Sheridan.

Sir Peter is painfully sensitive to this mockery – and is sufficiently likeable for us to care about his pain, as we are scarcely made to care for a Pinchwife or a Heartwell. Sheridan takes a big step away from the convention at this point, though never breaking from it. Sir Peter retains some of the complacent male chauvinism his stage predecessors took for granted, informing us in his long soliloquy in Act I.ii that he took great care to choose for wife a country girl 'who never knew luxury beyond one silk gown' but finds (no surprise to anyone else!) that she now behaves 'as if she had never seen a bush nor a grass plat out of Grosvenor Square'. This is the conventional lament of the erstwhile old bachelor. And there are other caricature elements: irascibility, impetuous judgements, an inclination to lay the law down which sets tiffs going again after they seemed to be made up, as in Act III.i, when he follows up a tender passage with a reminder to Lady Teazle to watch her temper, 'for in all our quarrels, my dear, if you recollect, my love, you always began first'. But he is also a man capable of humorous self-criticism. John Neville pointed this up with a little trick of stamping his foot to curb himself from some unwise outburst. The wrily humorous tone is dominant in the Act I soliloquy where he takes the audience winningly into his confidence (Neville spoke out from a pool of light to the fore of the open Olivier stage). They were invited to share sympathetically in a well known joke: 'When an old bachelor takes a young wife – what is he to expect!' By the end of his confession, however, he has made clear that softer human feeling is involved: 'the worst of it is I doubt I love her or I should never bear all this – However, I'll never be weak enough to own it.'

His real weakness, Sheridan hints, may be his tendency to think too much of what 'the world' says. Sometimes his unease on that score is natural enough. It is natural for him to shrink from the teasing he knows he will receive from the resolute bachelor, Sir Oliver, when they meet for the first time after his marriage. Sir Oliver does indeed react with robust mirth, though not to his friend's face. With only Rowley present, he allows himself to enjoy the joke with gusto:

> Ha, ha, ha! So my old friend is married, hey? A young wife out of the country. Ha, ha, ha! That he should have stood bluff to old bachelor so long and sink into a husband at last.
>
> (II.iii.1)

The balance Sheridan keeps between the broad comic convention and the new sensibility is charmingly demonstrated in what follows. Rowley has warned Sir Oliver that the marriage is a 'tender point' with Sir Peter. The friend takes heed and makes an effort to avoid wounding the husband's feelings, though, as his earlier laughter showed, he cannot help but hold the conventional view on its mistakenness: 'But what – I find you are married, hey? Well, well, it can't be helped, and so I wish you joy with all my heart' (II.iii). It is a totally truthful, if not altogether tactful, statement of his feelings. We laugh, and are touched by the effort to be both true and friendly. Insights of this kind into 'ordinary' complexities of feeling are what give *The School for Scandal* its deepest underlying seriousness.

The Teazle quarrels go on conventional lines: her extravagance, his parsimony, her restlessness, his staidness. One stock Restoration item, the possibility of the wife's taking a lover, had to be handled discreetly to conform with the eighteenth-century audience's sense of dramatic decorum – and the playwright's. Without a general conviction of Lady Teazle's sexual innocence he could not have ended the play with a hopeful reconciliation. Yet Sheridan also wanted to explore in the dangerous area, go further into it indeed than the Restoration satirists had done, or from a different angle, with more sympathy for the difficulties of both partners. The Teazles' verbal battles are witty and comic but require to be taken with some seriousness, as the opening episode of Act II. indicates:

Sir Peter: Very well, ma'am, very well. So a husband is to have no influence, no authority?
Lady Teazle: Authority? No, to be sure, If you wanted authority over me, you should have adopted me and not married me. I am sure you were old enough.
Sir Peter: Old enough! Aye – there it is.

(II.i.7)

His nagging sense of the discrepancy in their ages, a theme for mirth in Restoration comedy, creates a moment of poignancy here. The dry 'Aye – there it is' does not call for derision. This is the new sensibility epitomised in Kelly's *False Delicacy*, where similar sympathy is invited for fifty-year-old Cecil. Sheridan excels by his ability to keep his characters spirited and unsentimental even when he is exploring – with great delicacy – the 'embarrassments of the heart', in his own phrase. The balance of sympathy shifts continually and interestingly in the Teazle quarrels. Sir Peter cannot be blamed for suspecting his wife with Charles: Lady Sneerwell has provided false evidence of an affair, as the audience know. He has in fact behaved with restraint in keeping his suspicion to himself: only when enraged by his wife's taunts does he confront her with it. Yet she is entitled to be angry and we may have some sympathy with her fierce reply: 'You had better not insinuate any such thing. I'll not be suspected without cause, I promise you.'

It is a threat the audience may be expected to remember in Act IV.ii, when Lady Teazle complains to Joseph that Sir Peter is 'so peevish and suspicious' while she knows she is innocent. Typically Joseph seizes the opportunity, blandly suggesting that, as her husband should never be deceived in her, 'it becomes you to be frail in compliment to his discernment.' The screen scene is so amusing and spectacular in theatrical terms, we might underestimate the intricacy of its psychological substance. Thoughts, images, and fears from earlier scenes return in this more dangerous context, where half-meant impulses, like Lady Teazle's toward

revenge, threaten real disaster. With great panache Sheridan con-
trives a situation of sexual dalliance and anxiety, just close enough
to the edge to let loose a flood of deeper emotion from husband
and wife than they have ever allowed themselves to show before.
Paradoxically, it is this danger that saves their marriage.

The audience have a godlike view of all that is hidden from the
characters. When Sir Peter sits in Joseph's library, confiding his
doubts about his wife and Charles, we know she is not guilty, but
she might have been: her presence behind the screen shows she
can be tempted.[3] She is both innocent and guilty; her husband is
both right and wrong. There is a complex irony in the scenic
arrangement of speaker and listeners. Sir Peter pours his heart out
to a man incapable of really hearing him, while the unseen wife
hears what she was never meant to hear; that he can't help loving
her. Her possible deceit is contemplated sadly, without rancour.
How could principle hold out 'against the flattery of a handsome,
lively young fellow?'

Age is still a preoccupation, it is clear, but the whole tone of his
discourse has changed, seemingly under stress of imagining her
lost to him. Where once he chafed, he now makes a quiet statement: 'And then, you know, the difference of our ages makes it
very improbable that she should have any very great affection for
me.' Earlier grievances are brought into a new light. We recall the
scene where he scolded her for extravagance and she coaxed him
into giving her money, like an eighteenth-century Nora in an
upper-class English *Doll's House*:

Sir Peter: Ah, Lady Teazle, you might have the power to
make me good-humoured at all times.

Lady Teazle: I am sure I wish I had, for I want you to be in a
charming sweet temper at this moment. Do be
good-humoured now and let me have two hundred pounds, will you?

Sir Peter: Two hundred pounds! What, a'n't I to be in a
good humour without paying for it?

(III.i.179)

From his new perspective those requests for money look more
reasonable; he acknowledges the justice of her complaint in the
way he tells Joseph of it: 'She has lately reproached me more than

once with having made no settlement on her.' A conversion has occurred, a real change of heart, expressed in the dry language of money. The settlement he intends to make is 'truly generous', says Joseph, uneasy at the effect on the hidden listener.

He is right to be uneasy. But can we be convinced that Lady Teazle undergoes so full a conversion as she claims she has experienced, when she emerges from behind the screen: 'the tenderness you expressed for me, when I am sure you could not think I was a witness to it, has penetrated so to my heart that had I left the place without the shame of this discovery, my future life should have spoken the sincerity of my gratitude.' Critics have sometimes doubted this, as also the likelihood of the Teazles being happy as, Sir Peter says in the final scene, they 'intend' to be. It is not usually difficult, however, for the actors in performance to build up a relationship which promises happiness, even in the midst of the squalls. In Laurence Olivier's production there was obviously an underlying sexual attraction between his Sir Peter and the Lady Teazle of Vivien Leigh. She was responsive, even when most skittish and petulant, to the masterful, humorous personality under the tetchy middle-aged (not elderly) exterior. John Neville's Sir Peter drew a similarly promising response from his Lady Teazle for his quirky, charismatic character.

Diana Hardcastle's high-spirited, smiling Lady Teazle conducted the quarrels rather as a game, an amusing exercise, not so different from the dancing lesson she was enjoying (another of Wood's dumb show interpolations) when Sir Peter broke in with his 'Lady Teazle, Lady Teazle, I'll not bear it!' With the *Doll's House* analogy in mind, however, it would be possible to put more stress on her will to independence, the modern-looking aspect of her character. She is too young, too much a creature of her time to move far toward emancipation but the impulse can be felt – in her resentment at having to ask for 'every little elegant expense' and perhaps in her insistence on attending the Sneerwell salon despite Sir Peter's disapproval. Decorous, unmarried Maria frequents it too, so Lady Teazle's enjoyment of the 'school' is not to be taken as evidence of corruption. Wood's production had Maria in Act I enter running, to throw herself on Lady Sneerwell's bed, seeking sanctuary from her odious admirer, Sir Benjamin Backbite. There was a suggestion here that for both young women the louche, uninhibited atmosphere of the 'school' was a refuge from irksome pressures, including the normal restraints on free speech imposed by 'polite' society. Lady Teazle throws herself into the scene more robustly than Maria; as the wittier of the two, with a heavily restricted country upbringing, she can be seen as intoxicated by the chance to sharpen her wits among the smart set and literati (we are told that Snake, bad luck to the profession, is a writer and critic). Diana Hardcastle's laughing style was in tune with this concept, which is itself in tune with the radical elements in Sheridan's political philosophy, and his sympathy for young women struggling to assert their individualism. Lady Teazle uses frivolity and joking as a means to this end, though it is not until Act IV that Sir Peter learns how to read some of the remarks that previously outraged him, such as her deliciously faux-naïf riposte to his lecture on the extravagance of buying flowers in winter: 'Lord, Sir Peter, am I to blame because flowers are dear in cold weather? . . . I'm sure I wish it was spring all the year round and that roses grew under one's feet.'

At the same time, it is clear that she is at risk from the 'school'. She loses sympathy when she encourages Backbite to repeat stories about her husband and her entanglement with Joseph could have led to disaster, though she seems to have little real interest in him (she can be believed when she claims that she only wanted him in the first place as a *cavaliere-servente*). When the screen falls and everything has become clear, she is as sharp with herself as she has been with others. Her break with the scandalmongers is instant and final. She dismisses Sneerwell from her life in Act V with characteristic panache and forcefulness, playing wittily with the school metaphor by sending a message via their 'President' to that 'Scandalous college': 'Lady Teazle, Licentiate, begs leave to return the diploma they gave her.' She has resolved 'to kill characters' no more, a wording which indicates her advance in maturity.

Sir Peter has a harder struggle to extricate himself from the poisoned web. It is his weakness to think too much of what 'the Town' will say, so Sheridan implies. At key points throughout the play he is shown to be haunted by vivid imaginings of the 'paragraphs and ballads' the gossip writers will publish if they get word of his marriage troubles. He becomes violently agitated in Act V.ii by the waspish remarks of Candour and company (all the more venomous because they have been disappointed in their expectations by seeing him hale and well, not dying of sword or bullet wounds). 'Fiends! Vipers! Furies!', he shouts melodramatically after their departing backs. Worse, he is hampered in his deepest wish, to be reconciled with his wife, by vexing thoughts of the 'paragraphs about Mr S–, Lady T– and Sir P–' which readers of the gossip columns will find so very entertaining. A glimpse of Lady Teazle, charmingly in tears, off-stage, almost decides him to make it up but he still fears 'the Town'. If he allows himself to be reconciled, 'people will laugh at me ten times more'.

He receives the advice which puts him on the right path not from Sir Oliver (that mentor is too much amused by the upsetting of Joseph's image) but from the character whom Sheridan portrays as the most well-judging person in the play. True to the ethos of sentimental comedy, with its interest in wild young men and wise old retainers, and in line with his own republican instincts, Sheridan allots this crucial role to the servant, Rowley. It is he, when they are alone on the stage in Act V.ii, who plucks Sir Peter from the scandal quagmire with the classically sensible advice: 'Let them laugh and retort their malice only by showing them you are happy in spite of it.' They are the words he really wants to hear and he goes off to effect the reconciliation, though not before he has been tempted to let her cry a little longer: she does it so prettily and 'a little mortification appears very becoming in a wife'. Again, it is Rowley who puts him on the right road: 'Oh this is ungenerous in you'.

The dominating scandal motif is equally well integrated with the Surface brothers' plot. Here Sheridan was using a convention stamped with the sensibility of the eighteenth-century rather than the Restoration theatre. As in *The West Indian* and (more suggestively for Sheridan's purposes) *The Good Natur'd Man*, it involves the testing of a young man by a stern but benevolent elderly relative. Goldsmith had provided his compatriot with a demonstration of how this moralising convention could be turned to the needs of a subtle theatrical imagination. In Sheridan's hands the 'trial' situation becomes a vehicle for exploring a favourite region, where personalities split and multiply under pressure from some unknown source as well as from the more obvious demands of worldly self-interest. His focus takes in not one but two young men, placed in a curious relationship. The Surface brothers are opposites who are yet alike: strictly separated yet coming very close, even, at times, creating the impression of being elements in a composite whole. It is a more complex version of the world of masks and invented personae which was explored in *The Rivals* through the dual personality of Jack Absolute. There are, as ever, echoes of *commedia* and the Harlequin and anticipations now and then of a theatre to come; the floating identities on Wilde's stage; even, the pseudo-couples of Beckett.

An impression of separateness and contrast is overwhelmingly the first to be received. The brothers are kept physically separate for most of the play. Charles, as we noted, does not appear on stage at all until Act II.iii; he meets Joseph first in the following scene. Contrast is the essence here: one scene brings Charles a triumph, though he does not realise it; the next brings Joseph a catastrophe which he realises only too well. But though stringently separated in the flesh, the pair are continually juxtaposed in conversation, in ways which often seem to run their identities together. Sir Peter thinks Charles is the philanderer with Lady Teazle when in fact it is Joseph. Snake thinks it is Joseph whom Lady Sneerwell wants when in fact it is Charles. Joseph secretly pursues Maria who is committed to Charles. 'Interest' (meaning financial interest), Lady Sneerwell says bitterly, is his only motive. She may be right but the multiplication of links between the two brothers in the sexual sphere makes one wonder whether there is not also, at a deep unconscious level, the need to take over his brother's possession, 'be' him more completely.

There is a strange moment in the final scene (V.iii.61) when the brothers act in concert as though they really were one. Identity has become a very fluid and uncertain concept by this time. Sir Oliver arrives in Joseph's library to be identified by him as 'Mr Stanley', the poor relation he has already turned away once. When Charles appears on the scene and 'Mr Stanley' is reidentified as 'Mr Premium', careless Charles accounts for the oddity in terms of universal fluidity: 'I suppose he goes by half a hundred names, besides A.B. at the coffee-houses.' Each brother has his own angle on the Protean visitor but they are united in their need to get rid of him before he can blab to Sir Oliver. The stage picture at the point where they push and haul him through the door, as it opens on Sir Peter and party, is an image of conspiratorial closeness between the unlike siblings. The image lingers as the scene moves on. The brothers remain at one, listening with presumably equal mortification as Stanley/Premium, now metamorphosed into Sir Oliver, sums up what he has learned of their characters: from one, he says, he could not get a shilling, while from the rough handling of the other he stood a chance 'of faring worse than my ancestors and being knocked down without being bid for' (a neat conflation of Charles's embarrassments).

We wait for the brothers to respond but before they do there is a significant stage direction: '*Joseph and Charles turning to each other*':

> *Joseph*: Charles!
> *Charles*: Joseph!
> *Joseph*: 'Tis now complete.
> *Charles*: Very!

Like the stage direction, the cryptic little exchange seals the two off from the other characters in a play of their own: they seem for an instant to recognise the idea of their own performance: ''Tis now complete.' A curious impression is created of a single mind at work. The surfaces have touched.

Currents of attraction and repulsion run between the two opposite poles; Joseph, 'universally well spoken of' and Charles, 'the most dissipated and extravagant young fellow in the country'. The images are accurate as far as they go: not all the scandal at Lady Sneerwell's is fantasy like the absurd Laetitia Piper story. Charles *is* dissipated and extravagant, Joseph *is* widely thought of as virtuous and amiable. These are the stereotypes which the brothers have to live with. The interest for the audience is in seeing how they do this, what sort of gap exists between the stereotype and the full personality. In both brothers, not only in Joseph, much is hidden from the general view.

Charles is the character with the more obviously attractive qualities; candour, generosity, good-natured capacity to ignore offences (he is remarkably tolerant of Joseph's machinations in the eavesdropping episode of Act IV.iii). Sir Peter does not recognise his good points, partly, as Rowley says, because of jealousy, partly because he is influenced by the 'dissipated' image, so discreetly reinforced by Joseph at every turn. Sheridan evidently does not intend the audience to write Sir Peter off as a fool. Rather, his case is presented as paradigmatic of a universal difficulty in 'reading' character. An open, impulsive person like Charles is not necessarily easier to read than a more secretive one. Sheridan suggests this by keeping him at a distance from the audience; this also protects his attractiveness by not letting us get too close to see the warts. He is distanced by being brought late into the play, and by being always seen in public, never alone. Most significantly, he has no real love scene with Maria; no scene with her at all, in fact, until the final minutes of the play when they are surrounded by almost the whole company. There is a great stretch of his private thought on which no light falls.

The sympathy Charles arouses is somewhat equivocal too. He charms when he is being graceful and witty about his extravagances, as when he admits to making 'a little free with the family canvas' or says humorously that, although innocent of an affair with Lady Teazle, and averse to acting dishonourably, 'if a pretty woman was purposely to throw herself in my way – and that pretty woman married to a man old enough to be her father –' 'Well?', says Joseph eagerly. 'Why, I believe I should be obliged to borrow a little of your morality' (a wonderfully unconscious irony, with Lady Teazle behind Joseph's screen). But there are touches of a slightly coarser sensuality here and there, enough to suggest that the 'dissipated' stereotype is rooted in reality. Its sexual aspects are decorously concealed but show occasionally. There is a world of raffish experience in his greeting to Joseph in Act IV.iii (after difficulty in passing his servant): 'What, have you had a Jew or a wench with you?' A more disturbing trait is his willingness to cheat Jews and others by not paying bills. Sheridan encourages us to see this as a fault, though Sir Oliver is prepared to overlook it, by making Rowley, in Act IV.i, disapprove of Charles's refusal to put his creditors' rights before the needs of the poor relation, 'Mr Stanley'. Tradesmen don't count, for Charles: 'Justice is an old lame hobbling beldame, and I can't get her to keep pace with Generosity for the soul of me.' It is candid – and he is generous – but are candour and generosity enough? Goldsmith had raised similar questions with Honeywood, another 'extravagant young fellow' (as Charles describes himself). Sheridan leaves it to the audience to decide, but he points to a possible link between Charles's obduracy over settling his debts and his faintly complacent acceptance of his self-image. It is the 'extravagant young fellow' the scandalmongers gossip about who exits on the reckless line: 'So damn your economy, and now for hazard.'

We approach the truth of Joseph by an opposite route. In his case the public image is a deliberate mask which he holds in front of him to obscure his busy inner life. Ironically, we gain much closer admittance to the hidden self of the hypocrite who hides everything than we do to the open scapegrace who appears to have nothing to hide. In this paradox Sheridan's technique is seen at its most subtle.

Joseph's public face is on view from the moment he steps into Lady Sneerwell's room, paying a typically smooth, disingenuous compliment to Snake, against whom he will warn Lady Sneerwell once they are alone together: 'Madam, it is impossible for me to suspect a man of Mr Snake's sensibilities and discernment.' The mask seems to have become second nature – he has to be reminded by Lady Sneerwell that it is not needed with her: 'O lud, you are going to be moral and forget that you are among friends.' This immediately makes a game of the sentimental performance. We are encouraged to see it as just that, a performance, like the clever tricks of the Harlequin who cheats the credulous on the *commedia* stage. Joseph's response to Sneerwell has the cool impudence of the Harlequin in it: 'Egad that's true, I'll keep that sentiment till I see Sir Peter.' At the NT Jeremy Northam's personable Joseph made the most of the 'play' element, manipulating with élan the transitions between his personae which occur with brilliant rapidity throughout. His adroitness raised amused admiration (such as Charles Lamb felt for John Palmer, the actor who first played the part).

Where Charles is seen always from some distance and in company, Joseph is allowed to open himself up to the audience in a very intimate way, as a witty, sardonic observer, of himself as well as others. Peter Wood seized on the many opportunities offered by the text – and encouraged by the open spaces of the Olivier Theatre – to bring Joseph into the closest possible relationship with the audience. In Act II.ii, for instance, after his awkward triangular scene with Lady Teazle and Maria, he stepped forward, in a pool of light, very close to the stalls, to confide ruefully that somehow – 'I don't know how' – he had found himself Lady Teazle's 'serious lover' when he had only intended to ingratiate himself with her to further his cause with Maria:

A curious dilemma my politics have run me into. . . . Sincerely I begin to wish I had never made such a point of

gaining so very good a character, for it has led me into so
many cursed rogueries that I doubt I shall be exposed at last.
                                                    (II.ii.252)

This is appealing, despite the 'cursed rogueries'; or, perhaps,
because of his candour about them. For Joseph, like Charles, is
candid – though only with the audience, who are able to feel
themselves in a privileged position, enjoying ironic jokes closed to
those on stage. The asides which come thick and fast in the screen
scene turn Joseph into a quasi-hero:[4] it would be hard to resist
totally someone who keeps his head with such aplomb through one
crisis after another and shares his problems with such rueful
humour, as in commenting on Sir Peter's wish for secrecy about
the settlement he intends to make on Lady Teazle:

Sir Peter: . . . I would not have her acquainted with the latter
            instance of my affection yet awhile.
Joseph: Nor I, if I could help it.
                                                    (IV.iii.208)

Which is the 'true' Joseph, the calculating, self-interested poli-
tician, able so easily to slide into the unctuous, humourless rhetoric required by the sentimental role? Or the sharp, humorous,
self-observant being who takes us into his confidence, about his
mistakes and failings as well as his cleverness, questioning at the
very start whether his biggest mistake was not to saddle himself
with such a good character? He exits from the final scene exposed
and humbled but still endeavouring to preserve his public persona,
holding a few rags of rhetoric around him, to cover his nakedness.
Hypocrisy is uppermost as he struggles to tell a convincing story,
professing to be 'confounded' at discovering Lady Sneerwell's
treachery and resolved to follow her 'lest her revengeful spirit
should prompt her to injure my brother'. Is that how we are meant
to see him finally, as the exploded hypocrite? The comedy has
made it impossible to take so simple a view. Sheridan drew on
himself, his father said, to find the characters of the two brothers.
There is indeed a sense of some deep self-knowledge behind the
amusing, piquant and teasing multiplicity of personae the brothers
project between them – out of a relationship in which one can
never be fully separated from the other.
    The focus on 'sentiment' in the play has sometimes been taken

to indicate a rather narrow satirical intention. Sheridan, as always, enjoys a joke at the expense of the sentimental school. Sir Peter's cry from the heart – 'I never want to hear a sentiment again' – would have had extra resonance for an eighteenth-century audience familiar with the running argument over sentimental comedy. But the topical reference is incidental. The 'man of sentiment' is the agent of a much more general and timeless satire, to do with people's susceptibility to surfaces, their readiness to accept fine talk, stereotypes and clichés rather than test character for themselves, as Sir Oliver does.

Mention of Sir Oliver reminds us that the moral line is not straightforward. That wise judge forgives Charles for selling off his ancestors because he holds on to the 'ill-looking little fellow over the settee'. The repeated chant – 'But he wouldn't sell my picture!' – suggests that vanity looms rather large here (though of course Charles has convincingly demonstrated a capacity for good feeling, unflawed by intent to impress). Motives, even the best of them, are mixed: it is no good looking for total consistency. Such is Sheridan's ironic, tolerant moral, if a prevailing moral there has to be. Sir Peter is a much nicer character than Lady Sneerwell but he is taken in as she is not by Joseph's well-rounded sentences and is blind to Charles's virtues. The reason for this misjudgement is not simple either. Jealousy over Charles's supposed dalliance with Lady Teazle enters into it, as the ever-perspicacious Rowley points out. And this in turn stems from Sir Peter's debilitating anxiety over being so much older than his wife. It is not a black-and-white morality play though it is concerned with moral issues. The machinations of Lady Sneerwell cause a whole series of distortions, giving her the look of a standard villain at times. But she is humanised, as Peter Wood so effectively recognised, by being allowed to reveal glimpses of the genuine feelings seething under her hard, fashionable carapace: resentment at past ill-treatment (so she says) and fierce sexual passion for a man not interested in her. The motives of the other scandalmongers are not distinguished individually. Sheridan invites us to assume that they are quite ordinary and commonplace: boredom, desire for drama, envy and so forth. The gossips are the chorus, directed, as in classic convention, by a chorus leader who sees further than they do – Lady Sneerwell knows Joseph for what he is – but not far enough; she fails to detect Snake's treachery till he grinningly tells her at the end that although she paid him well to tell lies, he has been 'offered double to speak the truth'. As Sir Peter ignored good advice from Rowley, so she ignored Joseph when he warned her in Act I.i, to put no faith in Snake: he 'hasn't virtue enough to be faithful even to his own villainy'. He is 'a writer and a critic': a tart little in-joke.

Though painted in such bold, sparkling comic terms, it is a psychologically intricate and minutely observed scene of things that Sheridan has created in *The School for Scandal*. It is a masterpiece, as actors and audiences of every age have recognised, by virtue of being a sympathetic and truthful as well as brilliantly amusing comment on life's ironies and absurdities.

Notes

1. Sheridan and Goldsmith: Heavenly Twins

1. Peter Davison (ed.), *Sheridan: Comedies* (Basingstoke: Macmillan, Casebook, 1986), p. 10. NB: Additional page references to Davison are provided in the notes below for some quotations; his selection of extracts offers an illuminating conspectus of modern critical opinion.

2. Charles Lamb, 'On the Artificial Comedy of the Last Century', *London Magazine* (April 1822), reprinted in *Essays of Elia* (1823; London: Dent, 1906), pp. 165–72.

3. Laurence Olivier, in Folio Society edition of *The School for Scandal* (London, 1949), pp. 5–11 (Davison, p. 151).

4. George Bernard Shaw, *The Saturday Review*, 27 June 1895; reprinted in *Our Theatre in the Nineties*, II (London: Constable, 1932), p. 168.

5. Louis Kronenberger, *The Polished Surface: Essays in the Literature of Worldliness* (New York: Knopf, 1969) (Davison, p. 176).

6. Marvin Mudrick, 'Restoration Comedy and Later', in K. Wimsatt, Jnr (ed.), *English Stage Comedy: Six Essays* (New York: Columbia University Press, 1955), pp. 115–20 (Davison, p. 56).

7. Andrew Schiller, '*The School for Scandal*: The Restoration Unrestored', *PMLA*, 71 (1956), 694–704 (Davison, p. 157).

8. William Hazlitt, *Lectures on the English Comic Writers* (Oxford University Press: World's Classics, 1907), pp. 233–244.

9. A. N. Kaul, 'A Note on Sheridan' in *The Action of English Comedy* (New Haven and London: Yale University Press, 1970) (Davison, p. 104).

10. Mark S. Auburn, 'The Pleasures of Sheridan's *The Rivals*: a Critical Study in the Light of Stage History', *Modern Philology*, 72 (February 1975) (Davison, p. 109).

11. J. R. de J. Jackson, 'The Importance of Witty Dialogue in *The School for Scandal*', *Modern Language Notes*, LXXVI (1961) (Davison, p. 169).

12. Henry James, *The Scenic Art: Notes on Acting and the Drama, 1872–1901*, ed. Allan Wade (New Brunswick, N.J.: Rutgers University Press, 1948) (Davison, p. 144).

13. Horace Walpole, letter of 27 March 1773 to William Mason; in Rousseau, *Goldsmith*, pp. 118–19.

14. Charles Lamb, 'Artificial Comedy', p. 171.

2. The Lives and the Plays

1. Tom Davis, introduction to New Mermaids edition of *She Stoops to Conquer* (1979), p. xiii.

2. John Ginger, *The Notable Man: The Life and Times of Oliver Goldsmith* (London: Hamilton, 1977), p. 1.

3. Abbreviations used in the text: B = Boswell, L = Balderstone, both detailed in the Bibliography.

4. Joshua Reynolds, quoted in Ginger, *The Notable Man*, p. 32.

5. A. N. Jeffares, *Oliver Goldsmith*, Writers and their Work series (London: Longman, 1959, rev. 1965), p. 8.

6. Quoted in Madeleine Bingham, *Sheridan: the Track of a Comet* (London: Allen & Unwin, 1972), p. 209.

7. Review of *The Rivals* in *Morning Chronicle*, 30 January 1775. See Cecil Price (ed.), *The Dramatic Works of Richard Brinsley Sheridan* (Oxford University Press, 1973) (Davison, p. 83).

8. Cecil Price (ed.), *Sheridan's Plays* (Oxford University Press, 1975), p. xv.

9. Thomas Linley is quoted in James Morwood, *The Life and Works of Richard Brinsley Sheridan* (Edinburgh: Scottish Academic Press, 1985), p. 48.

10. Morwood, *Life and Works of Sheridan*.

11. Arnold Hare, *Richard Brinsley Sheridan*, Writers and their Work series (Windsor, Berks: Profile Books, 1981), p. 25.

12. Lewis Gibbs, *Sheridan* (London: Dent, 1947), p. 136.

13. Jack Durant, 'Prudence, Providence and the Direct Road of Wrong: *The School for Scandal* and Sheridan's Westminster

speech', *Studies in Burke and his Time*, XV (1973) (Davison, pp. 180–9).

3. The Plays in the Eighteenth-Century Theatre

1. For an illustrated account of the architecture and actors of the time, see Iain MacKintosh, *The Georgian Playhouse*, catalogue of exhibition at Hayward Gallery (London: Arts Council of Great Britain, 1975).
2. For an account of these epilogues see K. Balderstone (ed.), *Letters of Oliver Goldsmith* (Cambridge University Press, 1928).
3. I am indebted to Christopher Bauer for information on this point.
4. See Michael Kelly, *The Music of Pizarro*, and the various notes on the music by Cecil Price in his editions of the play.

4. Questions of Taste: Sentimental Comedy: 'The Good Natur'd Man' and 'A Trip to Scarborough'

1. Oliver Goldsmith, *An Enquiry into the Present State of Polite Learning in Europe* (1759), ed. A. Friedman (Oxford University Press, 1966), vol 1, pp. 154 ff.
2. Oliver Goldsmith, 'An Essay on the Theatre; or, A Comparison between Laughing and Sentimental Comedy' is reprinted in *The Good Natur'd Man* and *She Stoops to Conquer*, ed. George Pierce Baker, *Mermaid Drama Book* (New York: Hill & Wang, 1903), pp. 99–102. Also included is 'A Register of Scotch Marriages'.
3. Ibid., p. 99.
4. Ibid., p. 102.

5. 'She Stoops to Conquer'

1. See note 13, chapter 1.
2. The uninhibited behaviour of the servants made at least one member of the contemporary audience uneasy. His letter to Goldsmith included criticism of the 'drunken servant' called in by Marlow ('an unpleasing and surely an unnecessary character') and of the general 'impudence' of the servants, which, he said, was 'foolish and has a bad effect'.

3. Goldsmith's correspondent wrote: 'The audience should be made clearly to understand that the chaise is only stuck fast in the horse pond and not overturned.' See K. Balderstone, *Letters of Oliver Goldsmith* (Cambridge University Press, 1928) for this letter.

6. Sheridan's Comedy of Masks: Harlequins and Thespians

1. The sword is another link with the Harlequin, who conventionally carried a 'sword' (later known as a 'bat').

7. 'The School for Scandal'

1. Benedict Nightingale, *The Times*, 25 April 1990.
2. Peter Lewis, *Sunday Times*, 22 April 1990.
3. Ambiguity surrounds this episode. The servant indicates that it is not her first visit: "Tis her ladyship, sir: she always leaves her chair at the milliner's in the next street.'
4. Lamb admired the ability of Sheridan, and of the original actor, John Palmer, to win sympathy for Joseph's 'downright, acted villainy'.

Bibliography

Notes on Editions

The following editions of the works of Goldsmith and Sheridan have been used for quotation and reference:

Oliver Goldsmith

She Stoops to Conquer, ed. Tom Davis, New Mermaids edn (London: Benn, 1979).
Goldsmith: Two Plays, ed. George P. Baker, Mermaid Drama books edn (New York: Hill & Wang, 1931). Includes *The Good Natur'd Man*.

Richard Brinsley Sheridan

Plays, ed. Cecil Price (Oxford University Press, 1975).
The Rivals, ed. Elizabeth Duthie, New Mermaids edn (London: Benn, 1979).
The School for Scandal, ed. F. W. Bateson, New Mermaids edn (London: Benn, 1979).
The Critic, ed. David Crane, New Mermaids edn (Black, 1989).

The definitive editions of the playwrights' works are:
The Works of Goldsmith, ed. Arthur Friedman, 5 vols (Oxford University Press, 1966).
The Dramatic Works of Sheridan, ed. Cecil Price, 3 vols (Oxford University Press, 1973).

See *Bell's British Theatre* (London, 1796) for *False Delicacy* and other plays of the period.

Plays of the Eighteenth-Century Theatre, Everyman series (London: Dent, 1928) contains *The Clandestine Marriage*.

Select Book List

Balderstone, K. (*L*), *Letters of Oliver Goldsmith* (Cambridge University press, 1928).

Bingham, M., *Sheridan: the Track of a Comet* (London: Allen & Unwin, 1972).

Boswell, J. (*B*), *Life of Johnson* (London: Macmillan, 1893).

Davison, P. (ed.), *Sheridan's Comedies*, Casebook Series (Basingstoke: Macmillan, 1986).

Friedman, A., *Collected Works of Oliver Goldsmith*, Vol. 3, 'The Citizen of the World' (Oxford University Press, 1966).

Gibbs, L., *Sheridan* (London: Dent, 1947).

Ginger, J., *The Notable Man: The Life and Times of Oliver Goldsmith* (London: Hamilton, 1977).

Loftis, J., *Sheridan and the Drama of Georgian England* (Oxford University Press, 1976).

Morwood, J., *The Life and Works of Richard Brinsley Sheridan* (Edinburgh: Scottish Academic Press, 1985).

Nicoll, A., *A History of English Drama*, Vol. III, 1660–1900 (Cambridge University Press, 1952).

Price, C., *Letters of Richard Brinsley Sheridan*, 3 vols (Oxford University Press, 1966).

Rhodes, R. Crompton, *Harlequin Sheridan* (Basil Blackwell, 1933).

Rousseau, G. S. (ed.), *Goldsmith: the Critical Heritage* (London: Routledge & Kegan Paul, 1974).

Index